to Grow
for new and used Christians

Larry Richards

For new Christians.
For those who have been Christians for a while but aren't getting on too well.
For those who have been Christians a long time but something's gone sour.

Read it on your own . . . or better yet, study and discuss it with a group. Leader's Guide available from the publisher.

VICTOR BOOKS

a division of SP Publications, Inc., Wheaton, Illinois
Offices also in Fullerton, California • Whitby, Ontario, Canada • London, England

Ninth printing, 1978

Scripture quotations are from the *New American Standard Bible,* (NASB) © The Lockman Foundation, 1960, 1962, 1963, 1968, 1971, 1972, 1973, unless indicated otherwise. Other Bible versions quoted are *The Living Bible* (LB), © 1971, Tyndale House Publishers, Wheaton, Ill.; the *New Testament in Modern English* by J. B. Phillips (PH), © 1958, The Macmillan Company; and the King James Version (KJV). All copyrighted versions are used by permission.

Library of Congress Catalog Card No. 73-92609
ISBN 0-88207-708-2
© 1974, SP Publications, Inc.
World rights reserved.
Printed in the United States of America.

Contents

1 Fresh and New **5**

Part I NEW ATTITUDES

2 I'm Loved **16**
3 I'm Forgiven **27**
4 I'm Accepted **41**
5 I'm Not Alone **54**

Part II NEW PATTERNS OF LIFE

6 Little Daily Steps of Obedience **65**
7 Leaving It with God **78**
8 Life's Overflow **90**
9 Growing Together **101**

Part III NEW AWARENESS OF GOD

10 God, Our Father **114**
11 Jesus, Our Saviour **124**
12 The Holy Spirit, Our Companion **134**

1 | Fresh and New

Last night we met Tom.* He came to a small Bible study and sharing group we have every Tuesday. It was great to meet him; he's been a Christian for just a month now, and for him all of life is fresh and new.

Tom shared something of his life with us. How he'd left his east coast home three years ago, unsatisfied and searching. He'd rejected the teachings of his church long before . . . felt a despair with life that led him to think of suicide . . . had begun to dabble in spiritism in Phoenix. Then he met Jesus Christ.

Now for Tom life is new. His feelings and attitudes are changing. He's changing. God the Holy Spirit is working His miracles within.

New Creations

Meeting Tom, and welcoming him to our fellowship

---
* Each of the persons mentioned in this book is real. In most cases, names and places have been changed, but all other details are accurate.

of Christians, was a reminder that God really is at work in people. He is taking us and, in Christ, is reshaping our lives and our experiences to give us meaning and joy. He's proving in us the reality of what the Bible promises when it says things such as, "Therefore if any man is in Christ, he is a new creature; the old things passed away; behold, new things have come" (2 Cor. 5:17).

This is important for us to grasp, especially for new Christians. When you come to Christ, He gives you His life and you're *new*. Not only you, but everything about your life has become new. The old things have passed away: old attitudes, old ways of living, old feelings about yourself and others, all these things are simply unimportant and inoperative now.

Perhaps you've seen the Wizard of Oz on television. Remember when Dorothy was transported from Kansas to Oz? The cameras showed the transfer by photographing Kansas in black and white, and then filming Oz in color. It's to be like this for you as a Christian. You're to step out of your drab black-and-white existence and into a new world where life is in full color. All things fresh and new.

This newness is something the Bible states as a fact. But it's something of which we have to be reminded. Why? Because all that's implied by newness in Christ isn't something we experience automatically.

When a cocoon bursts, and the caterpillar that formed it emerges transformed, it doesn't have to learn to fly. The butterfly waits briefly for the sun to dry its wings, and then launches into flight.

But you and I have to learn.

In Christ we're transformed, yes. But we still need to learn to fly.

Tragically some Christians have never stretched their wings. They've never launched themselves into their new life. They've never learned how God's statement, "all things are new," can be realized in them.

The Old Remains

Ray was in his early 40s when life suddenly seemed to become too much for him.

He'd been a Christian since childhood, and attended a Christian college and seminary. For a while he taught Bible and education in a Christian college; then worked for several different Christian organizations. But now life seemed to overwhelm him: the truths he'd taught were a dream, and only the disappointments of his life a reality.

Ray had come to his present position with enthusiasm, and, using his natural creativity, had made several significant contributions to the ministry of his organization. But he'd reached a dead end: his ideas no longer seemed appreciated by his supervisors and his vision for the potential of the ministry was unshared by others.

At home, too, he was disappointed. Somehow his relationship with his wife had deteriorated. The strains were hidden and seemingly small, but they were there, deeply imbedded in the life they lived together but somehow did not seem to share. His children also discouraged him. One of his teens was rebelling; communication was breaking down with the others.

Ray's pressures and disappointments seemed so great that he was losing his ability to care. He couldn't make the necessary decisions on his job. He found himself putting them off, unwilling to accept the responsibility. He knew his attitude was affecting the people who worked for him, but he couldn't help it, and really, he simply didn't care.

He felt totally inadequate, weighed down, helpless, and lost.

Kay had entered the Christian life with the usual dedication she gave to everything she did. Always a leader and a strong personality, she put herself forward in church, and found that opportunities to take charge came quickly.

Kay was soon made chairwoman of a number of women's Bible study groups the church had started on weekdays. She used her many organizational skills well, drew together a team of group leaders, chose a curriculum and got the new ministry under way in a whirl of activity.

The next year Kay expected to chair the ministry again as a matter of course. So she was jolted when some of the women resisted her appointment. They seemed to want a "more personal" orientation to the studies rather than the thorough mastery of content Kay thought of as the only purpose of Bible study. They also seemed to feel that Kay was "insensitive," that in her dedication to the task she hurt others' feelings, and was too rushed to notice or to care.

The reaction angered Kay. How was anything going to get done unless some strong person took charge? Of course she took control and chose her kind of leaders and set the curriculum. Anything else would be chaos and anarchy. Kay knew her motives were only the best. She wanted to get God's work done and done right. And she *was* the best organized and strongest woman in the church. That wasn't pride speaking; it was simply a fact.

And so, hurt, but unwilling to admit it, Kay couldn't help the antagonism she felt toward the women who had questioned her leadership.

And she couldn't help wondering why, even though she kept so busy, she didn't feel happy in her Christian life any more.

Fighting down these feelings, Kay determined grimly to work harder at her task, overcome the "rebellion," and go on about getting the job done for the Lord.

Mal grew through most of his childhood with a birth defect that kept him from hearing or speaking. It was only at age eight that his trouble was diagnosed, and correction begun. School had been especially hard, but by his mid-20s Mal had completed two years of college, struggling, but doggedly working to prove he was able to learn and to succeed.

Personal relationships had always been hard for Mal; he'd been so different from his age-mates. Even in college he spoke with a kind of accent, like a person who learns a foreign language late in life.

To Mal, the message of Christ and new life in Him seemed an exciting way out of his loneliness and uncertainty. Mal had been led to Christ through the ministry of Campus Crusade. He now threw himself into Crusade evangelism. Using their interview approach and the four spiritual laws, Mal saw many guys and gals on his campus profess Christ.

Mal also immersed himself in Bible study. Plunging into the Word for three and four hours a day, Mal struggled to understand everything he could about the Scriptures. Particularly, Mal wanted to know what he must do to experience the joy he read of in the Bible and saw in the lives of some of his Christian friends.

Yet, whatever he did, the joy seemed to elude him. Desperate to see the miracles in his own life that he sensed in the lives of others, Mal determined to try even harder. He witnessed more and more, setting himself daily quotas to meet. He was afraid he wasn't spending enough time studying the Bible, so he stayed up later and later. And yet the joy continued to elude him.

One Sunday, Mal broke down and shared his bitterness with his fellow Christians. In tears he told of the jealousy he felt for those who seemed to experience God in their daily lives and could speak of their growing love for Jesus. He told of how hard he'd tried, and how unfair God seemed to be.

The promise of newness was unfulfilled.

Learning to Fly

Ray, Kay, and Mal each illustrate a peculiar paradox of the Christian life.

When you and I come to Christ, we are given new life. We're made new. But at the same time the old, *while "passed away" as far as its power to hold and control us is concerned,* remains a part of our personality. It is because of this that the Bible urges believers to *consider themselves dead* to all that characterizes the old life (see Col. 3:3-10), and to "put on the new self" which *"is being renewed."*

As Christians, you and I *can* go on living in the same old way. We can become discouraged, or bitter, or struggle compulsively to earn God's gifts, but we don't *have* to. We have the potential to go on to that fresh, full-color kind of life I noted at the beginning of the chapter.

The problems experienced by Ray and Kay and Mal were rooted in the fact that each of them tried to *live his new life by old principles.* Trying to live the Christian life while being governed by the feelings and values and beliefs developed over years of living without Christ led each of these people to tragic disappointment. *If you try to live your Christian life, guided by the principles that moved you before you came to Christ, you will lose out on the new.*

That's the reason for this book: to look with you at some of the "all things" that become new for us in Christ—the new feelings, attitudes, beliefs, and behavior we need if we are to "put on the new self" that *is* "being renewed" (Col. 3:10).

But before we go on to look at what transformation means for us, and how we learn to "fly," we need to sketch several things quickly.

Life comes first. There are many world religions, offering various pathways to human fulfillment. Christianity isn't this kind of thing at all. It's not something new to try—some promising philosophy or set of moral standards to guide behavior. Christianity is at heart a personal relationship with God. It's a personal relationship with God through Jesus Christ, who being God, entered our world as a human being (Phil. 2:5-8). He came to let us know what God is like, and how much God loves us. And He came to bring us a great gift, the gift of life.

Sometimes people assume that what they're already experiencing is life, and that it began at birth and ends at death. Actually, this is better described as "existing" rather than "living."

Recently newspapers told of a home in which the mother had chained her three children to their beds in a dark room shortly after each was born. When found, the oldest was a teen-ager . . . lying with the others, passive, naked, vacant-eyed in the bed that had been their world since birth. Cut off from all human contact, unable to talk, to develop, these individuals had existed—but had hardly lived.

The police who finally broke into their prison and brought them out into the world of men did, in a very real way, give them life.

It's something like this when we become Christians. The Bible pictures men as imprisoned by sin in a state of living death (see Eph. 2:1). We are born into the world, but we're trapped within the confines of the material universe, cut off from contact—not with other people, but with God. Yet it is just this, fellowship with God, that alone enables us to grow to our true potential as human beings! Created as we were in God's image (Gen. 1:26-27), the human personality only truly *lives* when relationship with God frees us to grow and become all that our Creator intends.

No wonder Jesus said, "I came that they might have life, and might have it abundantly" (John 10:10).

It was Jesus who broke into our prison to free us. And the Bible tells us that the act which secured our release was His death on the cross. Somehow in His death He took the full burden of every guilty thought and act of ours, and in exchange gave us forgiveness . . . and life.

This is the first prerequisite for experiencing the life we'll describe in this book.

You must *possess* new life before you can experience it. And your possession of life depends totally on your relationship with Jesus Christ, the Life-giver.

All new. The second thing to realize is that when we say we're going to look at life in a new way, we really do mean *new*. The Christian life isn't importing the "good" thoughts and values and feelings and ways of responding that we learned before. The Christian life involves a pervasive change in the way we look at ourselves and others and God. It's as far-reaching a change as that known by the three children who were suddenly brought out into the world of men. The old responses, the old ways of experiencing, are totally inadequate for the new. The changes we'll be thinking of are so pervasive that the Scripture's term, *"all things* are new," will be seen to be exactly true!

At the same time, as we explore, remember that your experience of new life is a progressive thing. You won't become an altogether different person. (It's really *you* that God loves.) But you will change, just as you grew from child to adult, remaining in one sense the "same person" but at the same time becoming new. So we'll be thinking about *growth*. About *becoming*. And we'll be learning how God has made it possible for us to experience all the joy of *being* renewed each day.

Not alone. Growth never takes place in a relational vacuum. God put us in families so that as children our personalities might be shaped by our relationship with our parents. God gives us husbands and wives to enrich and encourage continued growth. And to those who break into new life as Christians, God has given brothers and sisters—other Christians that He calls His church.

And we really do need a close and loving relationship with others if we're to grow as rapidly and joyfully as God intends.

So, please don't read this book alone—if you can help it. Study it with a small group of others, with another person, with whom you can talk and pray. And share your experiences as God in His grace works to give *you* all the joy of the new life that

Jesus died, and lives, to provide.

GOING DEEPER

To get the most from your exploration of life in Christ, talk about the following with a Christian friend.

1. What do you feel a "fresh and new" life for you would involve?
2. Pages 7-10 describe three people who have been Christians for some time, but who do not know "newness" as they should. Do you feel you are like any of these three? If so, describe how. If not, write out a brief description of a person who *is* like you, and share this with your friend(s).
3. To experience new life, a person must first *have* life, through a personal relationship with Jesus Christ (pp. 11-12). Share with your friend(s) how you became a Christian.
4. Bible study: Colossians 3:1-10.

PART I

NEW ATTITUDES

Christ's touch is deep and personal. Even our most firmly set feelings about ourselves and others soften and yield. In Christ you'll find the freedom to love and to be loved, to forgive and be forgiven, to accept yourself and others.

2 I'm Loved

Jan had always felt unloved and unlovely. Her parents worried that she might turn out as proud and flighty as other young people they saw and resented. So as she began to break into adolescence, they worked relentlessly to keep her humble.

"You don't need to look to see if you're beautiful," Dad would say if he caught her looking in a mirror. "I'll tell you if you're beautiful."

But he never did.

Even after she was married, Jan felt totally insignificant, unimportant, worthless. She saw her faults so clearly that one day, when asked in a Sunday School class to share "one thing you really like about yourself," Jan confessed that she couldn't think of a single thing.

Jan had been a Christian for many years. But she failed to grasp one of the most exciting realities that coming into relationship with Christ involves.

Jan failed to realize that she was loved. She didn't feel *special*.

You're Special

This is one of the first things that the Bible insists we realize about ourselves. Surprisingly, your specialness was a reality long before you became a Christian. Every human being is special.

Special as a person. The Genesis history of Creation gives us the first glimpse of our specialness. There we see God create a universe, fashion a world, and enrich it with life, all as a gift for His most special creation, man. It's only of man that God says, "Let Us make man in Our image, after Our likeness" (Gen. 1:26, KJV). And it was to humanity that God gave the privilege of using, subduing, and caring for the whole earth (Gen. 1:28-31).

If you wonder how special man is to the Lord, look through chapter two of Genesis and see how completely God planned to meet every human need: giving man responsibility, the opportunity to choose and act, meaningful work, beauty to enjoy, two sexes that we might know union, and a personal relationship with a loving Creator.

Everything recorded here helps us realize that to God, human beings are special. Of all creation before man, God's evaluating remark was "good." With this unique creation, man, added, God said, "very good" (Gen. 1:31).

Sometimes you may hear Christians argue that it's wrong to look at people as special today. Perhaps Adam was in God's image. But Adam sinned. And ever since, it is sin that is at the heart of human nature. Instead of seeing yourself and others as special, you ought to look at yourself with shame and rejection. You ought to feel *worthless*.

What such people are saying is that Jan's feelings about herself fit the facts, that when Jan could find nothing to like about herself, she was a model of what the believer's attitude ought to be toward himself and others.

This notion might have some merit if the expression, "God's image and likeness" referred to holiness. But, for a number of reasons, it doesn't seem that moral qualities were in God's mind when He spoke of likeness. Even after man sinned, God continued to speak of His "image and likeness" as a reality in humanity—distorted and warped, no doubt, but *there* (Gen. 9:6; James 3:9). So we have no basis for suggesting that the "image," the thing that made man special, was lost.

The Genesis passages that record the history of Creation don't stress holiness, but they do show over and over again that God prepared for man the fullest opportunity to express *personhood*. God performed works of creation; man was placed in a setting where, in subduing the earth, he too could express creativity (Gen. 1:28). God ruled and cared for His creation; man was also assigned rule over the earth. God spoke of beauty; man was given the capacity to share His appreciation for beauty (Gen. 2:9). *The thing that sets men apart from all creation is that men are persons, as God is.* In the capacities to think abstractly, to love, to make moral judgments, to have a sense of meaning or purpose, to choose, we are like God.

Personhood is not something that was lost in the Fall. Personhood is the stamp of the eternal on every human being who comes into our world. Because each human being is a person, bearing this likeness to the Creator, each person is special and important to God. You're special—and have always been special.

In the image of the Creator in each man, no matter how warped by sin an individual's personality may be, we can find much to appreciate and to love.

Special as a son. To affirm the specialness of every individual doesn't deny the fact of sin, or the tragic reality that apart from Christ men are cut off from God and under condemnation. The Bible even labels the non-Christian as an enemy of God, a person who has chosen to resist and rebel against Him. But what "special" enemies we've been! The Bible says, "God demonstrates His own love toward us, in that while we were yet sinners, Christ died for us." And it goes on to say that "while we were enemies, we were reconciled to God through the death of His Son" (Rom. 5:8, 10).

God alone understands the dreadful seriousness of sin. He faces the antagonism men feel for Him. And He loved His enemies enough to die for them. *To God, you were always special. Long before you knew or loved Him, He loved you.*

Yet, as a Christian now, you've become even more special to Him. From being a "special enemy" you've become a "special son." As a member of His family, you're even more an object of His love.

Probably, with me, you find it easy to love a child from the neighborhood. Probably we both choke with hidden tears over the newspaper report of an accident to a boy or girl or a crime against one. How much more deeply do we care about our own sons and daughters! Well, it's the same with God and you. He cried over you when you were only a stranger. Now that you're His child, He is filled with joy to hold you close.

Constant Love

There's a passage of Scripture that helps show just how special you and I are to God now that we're

His children. Why not follow along in your New Testament as we think about it. The passage is Romans 8:31-37.

Romans 8:31. The writer has reviewed all that God has done in bringing us into His family through Christ (vv. 28-30). How do we react when we realize that we really are special? Paul, the author of the letter, states it as a question: "If God is for us, who is against us?"

Jan's parents took a stand against her as a person. They tried to make her feel unimportant, worthless. But should Jan continue to let her father's view shape her feelings about herself? Or should Jan—and you and I—realize that all the negative, criticizing people who make us cringe and reject our specialness are *wrong!* The great and amazing fact is that *God* is *for* us. He stands against the critics and affirms. *"You are special. You are important to Me."*

Romans 8:32. How special are we? The specialness God demonstrated in creation fades to insignificance when we see our importance affirmed in Christ's death. God didn't spare His own Son. God gave Jesus, and Jesus offered Himself, to die for us. *You were so important to God that He gave His dearest and His best to bring you into His family.*

So never feel about yourself as Jan did about herself. Never feel you are worthless, that you don't count. God set His own price tag on you. And that price tag reads "Jesus."

You are worth His life—and death.

Romans 8:33-34. It's hard to feel important and valuable when we fall short of what we want to be or feel we ought to be. Yet we all do fall short. We let ourselves be pulled away from God, we dabble in sin, we feel our love for Jesus grow cold. And then we accuse ourselves and say, "See! I *knew* I was worthless. I knew I wasn't special. Because if I were special, I couldn't behave this way."

These verses in Romans warn us not to bring charges like these against ourselves. As a Christian you'll fail . . . often. And when you do, you'll feel guilty and bad about yourself. But God has taken care of that sin in Jesus' death. He has "justified" us—and that means both forgiven of sin and declared to be upright in God's eyes. He doesn't see you as a worthless sinner; Jesus continually intercedes for you.

God sees you as a child whom He loves.

We lose this perspective so easily because we're used to evaluating ourselves by our actions. If we do something warm and loving, we're "good." If we do something mean or angry, we're "bad." And we tend to feel ourselves valuable or worthless depending on how we're behaving just now.

But this very way of self-evaluation is one of those "old things" that passes away for us when we become Christians. In Christ we learn to look at ourselves from an entirely new perspective. Our specialness, our worth, our being loved, do not depend on what we do. We're special, worthy, loved, because of *who we are*. And who are we? Who are you? You are a person whom God loves and who He declares is special to Him!

The non-Christian often rushes about to earn acceptance with God by what he does. But the Bible says clearly that it is "not by works of righteousness which we have done." It is "by grace are ye saved through faith" (Titus 3:5, Eph. 2:8-9, KJV). God didn't decide to send Jesus because we had done something to cause Him to value us. It was all grace; and "grace" means God's own love flowing freely to us because He is love—*not* because we've earned

His appreciation. This Ephesians passage affirms that we are special because God loves us. The "faith" that saves is the realization that God accepts us *as we are* for Jesus' sake.

Abandoning works for faith is critical for salvation. And abandoning works for faith is to mark our Christian life as well. We need to realize that our worth rests in God's startling affirmation that we are special to Him. He loves us *for ourselves*. Not for what we do or fail to do.

When we realize this, we're freed from the ache of condemning and rejecting ourselves at each failure. We're freed to take God's point of view, to confess our sins and trust Jesus' intercession to cleanse us from them (1 John 1:9; 2:2). All the while we may rejoice that even in our failure we are still special.

We are still worthwhile.

We are still loved.

Jan realized this truth as we studied Genesis in a class I was teaching at our church. It not only freed her to value herself, it freed her to see her children in a different light. Like her own father, she had been focusing on her two preschoolers' faults, constantly criticizing and demanding. When she realized that God did not look at her to criticize but to express His love, she began to look for ways to help her boys feel special and loved too. She began to praise the special things they did and the growth they showed, and she took time to hold them close and tell them how special they were to her. Jan told us, "I want my boys to grow up *feeling* special and loved. I know how much it hurts to feel worthless. I want them to feel special to me and special to God."

This new way of living with herself and her children, not the old way, fits the biblical facts. We *are* loved and important. We *are* special, in ourselves, with all our faults and failings. How thrilling to relax and let ourselves respond to the freely-given love of our ever-loving God!

Romans 8:35-39. Paul has warned us against the inner feelings of self-condemnation that may keep us from realizing that God is *for* us. Now he assures us that absolutely nothing can ever separate us from God's love. We may have trials, difficulties, even tragedy. But this is never evidence of an interruption of God's love. *Nothing* will ever wedge itself between you and Jesus' love for you. The lines of love by which you're tied to God as His child can never be severed. You're much too special to God for Him to let you be torn away.

Unloved

If you wonder how important it is to start out your new life in Christ with a full realization that you are truly loved, think back to Mal, the collegian we met in the first chapter.

Mal's Christian experience has been marked by a frantic effort to prove to himself and to God that he is worth loving. Mal's expressed motivation for witnessing so constantly, for the hours of Bible study he's disciplined himself to do, is to see God working in his life and bringing him joy.

There's nothing wrong with a desire to know the touch of God on your life, or with a desire for joy. But to attempt to *buy* grace *is* wrong, because it rejects the fact of God's love for us and attempts to put our specialness on a merit basis.

Can you imagine going into a store and offering a nickel for a roomful of furniture? Can you picture yourself going to a car dealer and offering a dollar for a Cadillac? How then can we ever bring ourselves to go to God and insist He provide miracles on demand, holding out the copper coin of our own effort and insisting that what we have to offer is enough to pay for the great joy He has in store for us as His children?

It's even worse to imagine that we *have* to buy His love. Romans 8 says it. "How shall He [God] not with Him [Jesus] also freely give us all things?" (v. 32, KJV) God's gift of Jesus includes *everything*. And everything we receive from God comes as a gift. He *gives* to us because He loves us: fully, completely, totally.

Realizing this helps us see that the way to experience the newness God has for us is to recognize the greatness of His love, to accept the fact that we are special to Him, and to open our hearts in gratitude to accept the gifts He wants to give us.

Mal's compulsive effort to buy God's favor was a rejection of this whole understanding of our relationship with the Lord. Mal couldn't believe that God really loved *him*. Mal couldn't believe that he was special and worthwhile. He couldn't love himself unless he found a basis in his own works to feel some sense of pride. Mal could not open his heart to receive. He felt compelled to try to pay for what God wants to give.

Today Mal is in Europe. He went there as an evangelist—by faith, without support, and with no connection to a mission. He said he was going because he wanted to be in a place, so completely dependent on God, that God would *have to* do miracles for him.

How tragic!

How tragic that Mal still insists on trying to earn what God is so eager to give. How tragic that Mal cannot realize he is loved.

Love's Impact

Realizing that we are loved, and letting this realization soak into our personalities, has many implications.

The Christian who realizes his specialness to God is freed from destructive self-criticism. He's freed from struggling to earn God's gifts. He's freed, as Jan, to love others and to see them as special too. That critical, judging attitude that demands another *earn* love is going to be erased from his relationships with Christians and non-Christians alike.

Accepting the fact of your own specialness and *feeling* loved is a basic first step toward becoming a loving person. A Christlike love is only possible for one who shares Christ's attitude toward human beings. And that must begin with an attitude toward ourselves of acceptance and joy at our specialness and a full confidence that we are loved.

Actually, this is the focus of one of the Bible's richest prayers for believers: that we might realize how loved we are. Read it here, from Ephesians 3:17-19:

> I pray that you, firmly fixed in love yourselves, may be able to grasp (with all Christians) how wide and deep and long and high is the love of Christ—and to know for yourselves that love so far beyond our comprehension. May you be filled through all your being with God Himself! (PH)

Picture it, if you will.

You're standing on a hill, with all creation stretched out around you. You look to each horizon. As far as you can see it stretches, a shimmering mantle of God's love. You look up; you peer down. It's there, everywhere, enfolding you in the center of a love that has no limits and no end. *That* is the "breadth and length and height and depth" of God's love for you.

You stand there now.

In the very center of God's love.

GOING DEEPER

1. Make a list of the things that you truly like about yourself, and share these with your friend(s).
2. Was your childhood like Jan's? If you've grown up not feeling special or worthwhile, talk about the influences that shaped your feelings with your friend(s).
3. Look through the chapter again, and jot down notes on how God feels about you.
4. Look at Romans 8:31-39 and Ephesians 3:17-19. Try memorizing them, and think about the meaning of each phrase this week, thanking God that you really are special to Him.
5. Bible study: Genesis 1—2; Romans 5:6-11.

3 I'm Forgiven

Of all the old feelings that hang on to distort our new life in Christ, one of the most deceptive is guilt.

Rob has been a pastor for over 11 years; yet frequently he's thrown into despair by feelings of guilt, triggered by the slightest failure. Often he finds that his sense of guilt is what spurs him on in his ministry. Without it, he wonders if he'd get much done. But still his nagging sense of shame, and the agony of feeling himself a failure, rob him of much joy.

Rob's experience points up two of the many ways that false guilt distorts the lives of Christians. When Christ promised "abundant life" He wasn't referring to despair! And, God wants love, not guilt, to move us.

What About Guilt?

I used the words *false guilt* in referring to Rob. Does that mean that guilt isn't real? That it's only a subjective feeling that we're to rationalize away? Not at all. The Bible says clearly that guilt is a very real thing. But Bible guilt isn't "guilt feelings"; it's actual guilt, incurred by specific acts of sin.

So before we can think meaningfully about guilt, we have to be clear on sin. There are many Old and New Testament terms that give depth to our concept of sin. According to Scripture, "sin" can be viewed as error, failure, trespass, transgression, missing the mark, going astray, even rebellion. A glance at this list makes two things clear. In some instances, sin is closely related to imperfection. In others, it's related to willful choice.

Imperfection. We "miss the mark," not necessarily because we aren't shooting at it, but because we simply aren't skilled enough to hit it.

You've probably experienced this in your life. You've wanted to do something to help someone. You've wanted to show love. But you've chosen the wrong way to do it. The result: both you and the other person were hurt. Somehow, though the target was acceptable, your aim was poor! This is part of what the Bible means when it says we're sinners.

Recently I met a young woman with a smiling face, a tall and willowy body . . . and arms shortened to withered stumps. Her mother had taken thalidomide during the pregnancy, and the daughter was born deformed. In just the same way, you and I have been born deformed, affected by something done by our first parents long before our birth. Because of sin's distortion of our personality, we do fail. We do make errors. We do miss the mark and go astray. And when we do, we realize with shame how grotesque and misshapen *we* are, twisted by a sin that is the common heritage of all humanity.

Willful sin. Yet there's another dimension to sin, one shown in words like *trespass, transgression,* *going astray,* and *rebellion.* These words point to an active choice of the will. This too is a part of what sin means. Each of us has chosen and will choose to do things that we know are wrong. We rebel against what is right, and against the God who reveals right to us.

No doubt, this is something you have experienced. Often your *motives,* not just your aim, have been wrong. When you choose the wrong target for your actions, "sin" takes on a personal and volitional dimension.

According to Scripture, both these kinds of sin make us *guilty.* (Note that I'm not saying here that sin makes us *feel* guilty, but that we *are* guilty.) In Romans 3:19 the word translated *guilty* means *under justice.* In Matthew 23:18, *guilty* speaks of indebtedness, of owing. In four other New Testament passages the word translated *guilt* emphasizes that because of sin we are *under* or *subject* to something. In two of those places, what we are subject to is said to be death.

So if, like Pastor Rob, you feel despair and shame at times when you shoot at a good target but miss, or when you spend your effort on a target you know is wrong, those feelings are in harmony with the fact that sin has made you guilty. Guilt feelings would seem to fit the fact, only too well!

Guilt, Why?

When we think back to the fact that God loves us— *really* loves us—we begin to wonder about guilt and guilt feelings. Love certainly doesn't design life to drive us to shame, failure, and despair! What is the role of guilt in a person's life? And how do we handle it?

Actually, God didn't give us a sense of guilt to torment us but to alert us to the reality of sin. If you inadvertently brush against a hot burner, immediately your body cries out in pain. Warned, you jerk your arm away. But medical history records some people who cannot feel pain. When their arm touches something harmful, there's no warning. Often they are seriously injured because they can't tell they're being hurt. Guilt feelings do for the heart what pain does for the body. God has programmed feelings into our personalities to warn of the reality of a sin which can destroy us.

John joined our Bible study group just yesterday. At the end of our meeting, he was invited to share something about himself, and his story just seemed to burst out. He shared how he had been thrust out of his church 13 years before because of his marriage to a Protestant. Unable to go to confession or receive the sacraments, his sense of guilt began to build up over the years. Following the breakup of his marriage, the burden of guilt and failure was almost more than he could stand.

Then a visitor from a Baptist church invited him and a neighbor to a singles' fellowship. John went and that first night heard the Gospel of God's love and forgiveness. He was impelled to go forward at the invitation, but resisted. After all, you don't "join a new religion" until you've studied it.

In two more meetings with the group that week, God touched John firmly with the Gospel message. John went forward and received Christ as personal Saviour. He went home with a sense of total freedom. He knew that his guilt was gone, that he was now a forgiven man.

Guilt had been an awesomely painful burden to John for years. But that very sense of guilt that hurt him so much was what God used to bring him to Jesus.

This is a basic thing to get in mind about guilt. *It should always direct our attention to Jesus!*

Direction

Many Christians have shared John's experience in coming to Christ and learning the joy of forgiveness. But too many have forgotten the implicit lesson as they have moved on into the Christian life.

Jackie came from a home where there was no love, only bitterness and antagonism. At first she'd surrendered to despair and simply refused to try to do anything worthwhile. Later, when she found things she was good at, such as making her own clothes and other at-home tasks, she developed great pride in her abilities.

At her conversion, Christ brought Jackie an initial sense of freedom, but that soon disappeared as she found she was still a failure in many areas—particularly when it came to reaching out and making friends. These failures made her feel both ashamed and guilty. But rather than let her sense of guilt direct her attention to Jesus, she let it focus her attention on herself and on the things she could do well.

Soon she found herself looking with contempt on women who weren't as creative as she, or as good around the house. She began to look closely at other people to find their faults and weaknesses, so she could reassure herself about her superiority to them. Soon all the antagonism that her mother had exhibited toward her marked Jackie's feelings toward others. She had become a self-righteous person: someone who tried to handle guilt by hiding her own weaknesses, emphasizing her accomplishments, and downgrading others until she could feel that she stood "above" them.

That's what I meant at the beginning of the chapter when I said that of all the old feelings that hang on to distort our new life in Christ, guilt is the most deceptive.

Guilt can rob you of the joy of doing things out of love for Jesus.

Guilt can turn you into a hardened, self-righteous person.

Guilt can rot away the joy that knowing Jesus is meant to bring.

But guilt is not meant to do any of this! Instead, God means guilt to do one simple thing in our lives: direct our attention to Jesus.

Forgiveness

When John returned to his bachelor apartment after accepting Christ, his sense of release and freedom was a reflection of reality. His guilt had been real. But so was his forgiveness. When John met Jesus at the cross, the Lord accepted John into His family and forgiveness wiped out his guilt.

It's important to realize that guilt directs attention to Jesus *for forgiveness*.

Of course, sometimes we may feel guilty even when we really aren't. If we've been raised to view something as wrong, feelings of guilt may persist even after we come to the conviction that the matter in question does not involve sin in any way. This "guilt," too, we must bring to Jesus. Not that we confess as sin that which is innocent, but we need to bring our feelings and convictions into the light before the Lord so that we are at peace.

In the New Testament, "guilt" is mentioned only 6 times—and only 16 times in the Old. But 60 times in the New Testament alone God speaks of forgiveness. In most of these cases, forgiveness is directly related to sin, which is the root of guilt. God doesn't only deal with guilt, the result. In Christ He has dealt decisively with sin, the cause!

The words translated "forgive" are fascinating to explore. In the Old Testament, the major word means, literally, *to send off*. Psalm 103:2-3 blesses the Lord as One who *pardons* (literally, *sends off*) all our iniquities. And Jeremiah promises in the coming Christ that "I will forgive [*send off*] their iniquity, and I will remember their sin no more" (Jer. 31:34, KJV).

The New Testament picks up the same theme, with one word that emphasizes *be gracious to* and another that restates the Old Testament term: *send off*. So God says, "Be kind to one another, tenderhearted, forgiving each other, just as God in Christ also has forgiven you" (Eph. 4:32). Instead of responding to sin with the judgment it deserves, God has determined to be gracious. He reaches out in love to touch the sinner. Touching us in love, He *sends off* our sin.

This is why we come to Jesus when we sense guilt. Jesus continues to *send off* sin. He knows our inadequacies and how prone to failure we are. He touches us, and sends away our weaknesses. Jesus knows our perverseness and how quick we are to turn to our own way. He touches us, and sends away the results of our willfulness and the willfulness itself. *And then He remembers our sins no more.*

Rob torments himself with the memory of his failures. But God has already forgotten them.

Jackie couldn't face herself and her failures, so

she buried them deep within her personality. But God wants only to send them away: to help her forget the times she's stumbled and fallen.

Others struggle to "do better," sped by the yapping dogs of remembered guilt. But God wants us to seek forgiveness, and then to forget our sins just as He has forgotten them.

Something that often troubles new Christians is their continuing need to have sins "sent off." There's an initial glow that many experience in salvation, a glow that seems to promise total freedom from the inadequacies we've known and from the pull of evil desires. It's a jolt when we discover that after coming to know Christ the old weaknesses are still there. The old driving desires to do what is wrong still push and pull at us.

Sometimes the first fall—that first act that you thought you just *couldn't* do again—brings all the old feelings of guilt and worthlessness washing over you again. No wonder some people get discouraged early in their Christian life—and simply abandon trying to grow.

But the Bible faces this question head on and warns us not to be surprised when we sin after salvation. The Apostle John puts it very boldly in his first New Testament letter. "If we say that we have no sin, we are deceiving ourselves, and the truth is not in us" (1 John 1:8). If we say the inadequacy is gone, we only fool ourselves. If we say the desire for wrong is gone, we only deceive ourselves.

Both inadequacy and the tendency to want what is evil are deeply ingrained in our personalities. They hang on grimly, even after new life has come. So the fact that we "have sin" is something we're to face head on. Something to recognize and to admit.

And then turn our attention quickly to Jesus! Thus John continues, "If we confess our sins, He [Jesus] is faithful and just to forgive us our sins and to cleanse us from all unrighteousness" (1 John 1:9, KJV).

Even after conversion, we, for John is speaking here to believers, do sin. But we can face our sins, so that the guilt will be gone. We'll be free to forget them and the disappointment they brought, even as God forgets. Second, He will "keep on cleansing us" from all unrighteousness. With sin and guilt gone, God will be able to get on with the business of making us more and more like Him.

There's an incident in Luke's Gospel that illustrates the principle John has presented here (Luke 5:18-26). It tells of a man brought to Jesus on a stretcher and let down through the roof of a home where the Lord was teaching. In response to faith, Jesus said to the paralyzed man, "Friend, your sins are forgiven you" (v. 20).

Immediately the onlookers began to think, *Just a minute! Who can forgive sins? Only God! To have a mere man pronounce forgiveness is blasphemous.*

Jesus knew what they were thinking, so He asked them whether it would be easier to say "You're forgiven," or "Get up and walk."

The obvious answer is that it's far easier to say, "You're forgiven." After all, there's no way to *prove* whether that forgiveness is real or not. But if you say "get up," there is going to be clear evidence of just how much power you have. If the person doesn't get up, you've been shown up as a fraud.

So Jesus turned again to the man and said, "Take up your stretcher and go home." *And the man got up!* Jesus demonstrated the power of His forgiveness not only by touching the inner man, but also by overriding his physical incapacity. He forgave *and* gave the power to walk.

This is what John is promising us when he says that when we confess our sins to Jesus, He forgives our sins and cleanses us from all unrighteousness. *He sends away our past failures, and He gives us power to walk a new life!*

Learning to live as a forgiven person, then, is utterly vital to your new life. When you feel guilty, or know that you've sinned, turn to Jesus right away. Don't wallow in shame. Don't pretend, and build walls of self-righteousness to hide your failures. Don't even try harder to make up for what you've done or haven't done. Come to Jesus right away to confess your sin. And realize that when you do face sin this way, Jesus sends off your sin *and* pours new strength into you for that new life He's given you to live.

When sin has been confessed and forgiven, *forget it*. And get on with the business of living for Jesus!

I'm Forgiven

Realizing that "I'm forgiven" goes a long way in changing our approach to living.

One thing it changes is our motives—and this is critically important. All of us have been pushed at times by unworthy motives into good actions— actions that may even have turned out well. Rob has often been moved to pastoral action by a sense of guilt. God has often blessed. People he's visited have come to know the Lord. Others with whom he's counseled have been helped. He often wonders if he'd have accomplished as much for the Lord if he hadn't been pricked into action by guilt.

Yet there's something that all of us miss if our actions are motivated by guilt or by a sense of obligation. What we miss is the *blessing to ourselves* in being used by the Lord.

In the Bible's great "love" chapter, 1 Corinthians 13, something is said that is often misunderstood. "If I give all my possessions to feed the poor, and if I deliver my body to be burned, but do not have love, it profits me nothing" (v. 3). Now, certainly such a gift would profit the poor. They would benefit from the action no matter what its motives. We have a parallel thought in Philippians 1, where Paul notes that some who preach Christ do so from questionable motives. But the preaching of the Gospel still profited those who heard and responded—no matter what the motives of the preacher were. So God can use our actions whatever may move us.

Yet, while others may benefit from such actions, *we do not*. Any actions not motivated by love "profits *me* nothing!"

Remember Mal from chapter one? He hurried so to *do* for God. He witnessed vigorously, and people responded to the Gospel. But he still felt empty inside. An intense and self-centered need to prove that he was worthy motivated his actions—not love for God or love for the people he contacted. God used his actions to benefit others. But it profited *him* nothing.

In Phoenix we depend on canals to bring us water for irrigation, for drinking, for existence. One kind of canal I've noted since living here is cement lined —a thin shell of concrete covers the inner surface, and the water flows through it to the thirsty land beyond. Another kind of canal has no concrete lining. The water flows through this canal too— but some water seeps into the ground as it passes.

Around this second kind of canal all kinds of life flourish. In bringing life-giving water to the land beyond itself, the channel participates in the gift.

It's like this with us and God's love. There are Christians whom God uses to channel His love to others, who still feel dried up and destitute themselves. Their lives are lined and brittle with guilt and duty. There are others whose lives are marked with the freshness and vitality of the Spirit's fruit and presence. Their lives have been made porous and open to His touch—by love.

As we learn to accept forgiveness from God for our failures and guilt, and as we learn to live with joy in that forgiveness, our love is aroused more and more. *And that love will move us, far more effectively than guilt, to reach out to others for Jesus' sake!* So it's vitally important to realize, "I'm forgiven." And to let each twinge of guilt direct us back to Jesus for a fresh touch of that forgiveness which sends our sin away and opens us to cleansing and renewal.

Learning to accept forgiveness is closely associated with learning to extend it. And don't misunderstand this: we are to live with others as God lives with us.

Other people are as inadequate and prone to failure as we are. Other people are as susceptible to the impulse to do evil. Shall we respond to them in anger and judgment (our natural reactions, especially if we bear the brunt of their sin), when God has responded to *our* sins with forgiveness? No wonder the Bible calls upon us to bear with one another, and forgive (be gracious to) one another, whenever one has a complaint against another; just as the Lord forgave us, so also should we (see Col. 3:13).

It is a great relief to be freed from the dreadful tension of expecting perfection in other people. It is wonderful to accept people as they are, and to approach them with the free offer of a relationship based on God's kind of forgiveness. Not with the demand they improve (the "ought"), or with an insistence that they be ashamed (the guilt). Through forgiveness, we unlock all of life to God's cleansing and transforming power.

You'll find as you grow in Christ that understanding His forgiveness and living as a forgiven person has even greater implications than those we've explored. But for now, think just a while on these great truths, and what forgiveness means to you.

Have you been disappointed in yourself and ashamed of your failure to follow Jesus as fully as you wish? You're forgiven.

Have you made choices that you knew were wrong and come to feel that you've lost all right to hope for God's mercy? You're forgiven.

Have you pushed yourself to do the "right thing" because you felt you ought to, or to avoid the anguish of guilt? You're forgiven.

Have you built walls of self-righteousness to protect you from the failures you're too ashamed to face and to admit? You're forgiven.

Have you been bitter and critical of others, disappointed in them and angry at them at the same time? You're forgiven . . . and so are they.

So live as a forgiven person.

When you feel the touch of guilt, bring it to Jesus. Let Him send the sin away and stand you on your feet to travel on in your new life. Thank God for His great gift of love and for His forgetfulness of all that's base and weak about you. And let your own awakening love for Him speed you on to cleansing and to joy.

GOING DEEPER

1. Has accepting forgiveness been easy or hard for you? Why? Share your experiences with your friend(s).
2. Look through the chapter again, jotting down from the text and quotations what the Bible teaches about sin and forgiveness. Which of the truths listed have you already understood and been counting on? Which are new to you?
3. A key passage for memorization is short but tremendously significant. It's 1 John 1:8—2:2. Meditate on it this week—and practice it.
4. Talk over the practical implications of living in God's forgiveness, as brought out on pages 36-39. See if you can draw illustrations from your own or others' experiences.
5. Bible study: Matthew 18:21-35.

4 I'm Accepted

Bob was feeling totally discouraged. For two years he'd thrown himself fully into the Christian life. The youth minister at his church, who had come to know him intimately, characterized Bob as a guy who really wanted to do God's will—more than anything. Others too saw real growth and many marks of Christ's presence in Bob's character and in his zeal for Christ.

Why was Bob discouraged? It seemed to him that he wasn't growing *fast enough*. He wanted to be more mature as a Christian than he was.

The desire to grow out of our old selves and into the new persons Christ makes possible is natural, a desire you'll feel intensely if you haven't already. And it's a healthy desire. But unless you understand how spiritual growth takes place and learn to accept yourself at each stage of this life-long process, you can become discouraged too. We all need to learn to do something that's very hard: *we need to learn to value ourselves as incomplete . . . and yet fully accepted.*

The Power of Love

Sometimes people misunderstand what we've been saying in the last two chapters. "God loves you as you are," or "God forgives you" sounds like an awful compromise. To some, it suggests a willingness to settle back and be satisfied with shortcomings rather than seeking change. They somehow fail to realize that counting on God's love, welcoming His forgiveness, opens the doors of the personality to dynamic growth. It's *love*—not guilt or dissatisfaction or shame—that has power to change a person for the better.

This is something that we need to understand clearly. God *is* set on changing us. He didn't rescue us from our old way of life simply to let us settle back hopelessly into it. In His very first touch on your life, He had transformation in mind.

Scripture makes very clear what this transformation is. Put most simply, it is becoming like God not only in personhood but in holiness. So the Apostle Peter urges us, "Like the Holy One who called you, be holy yourselves also in all your behavior; because it is written, 'You shall be holy, for I am holy'" (1 Peter 1:15-16). A little later in this New Testament letter, God shares the reason holiness is possible. "You have been born again," and as Phillips paraphrases it, "the live, permanent Word of the living God has given you His own indestructible heredity" (1 Peter 1:23, PH).

You can be like Christ because His life is in you!

This same thought is often expressed in the Bible, from Christ's gentle insistence that we model our attitudes and actions on the Father rather than men (Matt. 5:48), to Paul's joyous realization that God has destined us to "become conformed to the image of His Son, that He might be the first-born among many brethren" (Rom. 8:29). Far from settling for what we were when He first touched us, or for what we are now, God intends that we should be like Jesus!

So when God tells us that we are loved, and that we are forgiven, He hasn't abandoned His purposes for us; He hasn't consigned us to stumbling and failure. Instead, God uses love and forgiveness to free us from the old and set us on the way to being new.

Incomplete but Accepted

Sometimes while we're on the way toward Christ-likeness, we become discouraged. Like Bob, we want to be—and we feel we ought to be—farther along than we are.

I have a 10-year-old son, Tim, who looks up to his teen-age brother, Paul, and tries to do the same things Paul does. Usually he can; Tim's a well-developed child. But every now and then there's something he can't do as well, and it frustrates him terribly. He sees Paul driving for the basket and making a reverse lay-up. When he tries, too often the ball won't go in. So Tim gets frustrated and upset. Paul shoots his air pistol with great accuracy. Tim's getting good, but he's not good enough. Paul, who plans to be an artist, can draw and paint with great skill. Tim is good for a 10-year-old, but his pictures don't look like Paul's.

It's so hard for Tim to realize that age and experience account for these skills of Paul's. And that he can't expect to do everything as well as a teen-ager.

Age plays a part in the Christian's life too. It's through time that we mature as we gain more experience of God's ways. As Hebrews 5:14 says, the "adult" believer is the one who "has developed by experience his power to discriminate between what is good and what is evil" (PH).

I try to help Tim accept himself *as he is*. But it's hard when he so badly wants the results of the growth process—without having to take the time to grow!

In a way, all of life testifies to us that we are to accept ourselves as incomplete, and to be glad for our present stage of development.

Tommy, the baby next door, is just a year old. He's beginning to walk now, delighted to stumble after new and old fascinations, intrigued by the little black carpet beetles that seem to find their way into every Phoenix home. It's a joy to see Tommy splash in the pool, or gurgle with delight when presented with someone's toe to play with. Tommy is very immature—just a baby. But he's delighted with life as he finds it, thrilled with the new experiences of walking, eager to learn more about the things and people that make up his ever-expanding, interesting world.

Tim, our son, is a probing 10-year-old. His hobbies so far this year have included rock polishing (using stones he picks up on our trips around Arizona), snakes, and, right now, astronomy. He's subscribed to *Sky and Telescope,* earned money for a good refractor telescope set on an equatorial mount. During the summer nights he's been staying up late, exploring the sky, studying Jupiter and its four flashing moons, the Pleiades, and many other mysteries. He does get frustrated about many things he can't do yet—but still he throws himself intensely into exploring the fascinating mysteries of our universe.

Paul is 17, built solidly for the wrestling and the daily weight lifting he enjoys. An avid reader, Paul devours historical books and stories, paints pictures that have deep and personal meaning for him, and shows traits of steadfastness and willingness to work (balanced of course by a somewhat relaxed approach to life) that give his parents some insight into the man he's going to become.

Each of these persons is a delight to us. It's fascinating to see each grow, to see each *becoming,* to thoroughly enjoy each one as an individual who is incomplete, but, oh, so accepted.

We aren't disappointed in Tommy because he can't talk astronomy.

We aren't disappointed in Timothy because he can't paint professional oils.

We aren't disappointed in Paul because he isn't ready yet to leave home and take up adult life.

Incomplete, yes.

But accepted. And loved.

The point, of course, is simple. All our lives you and I will be, as our children are, incomplete—but accepted. We'll never reach the goal of full Christlikeness. Not until we see Him at His coming (1 John 3:2). But our life is to be one of *growth toward* Christlikeness. At first we'll be babes—stumbling and falling, reaching out curiously and fumblingly to touch things we shouldn't. But we'll be loved by our Father. And accepted.

Later we'll be like that 10-year-old. Fascinated by the wonders of our new world, exploring, but unready yet for commitment to a special path that may be our life's ministry. We'll look then at older Christians and be angry and frustrated with ourselves at times. Childlike, we'll be bored and unhappy at times too, as well as intense or totally preoccupied with others. But we'll be loved by our Father. And accepted.

Looking backward, we'll be able to see that we are no longer what we were. Looking forward, we'll see that we're not yet what we'd like to be. Yet when we look at ourselves now, we need to realize that we aren't to be ashamed or self-satisfied. We're to rest in the fact that we're loved by our Father as we are. We're accepted.

Growth

How then do we grow? In one place Jesus spoke to worriers, those people who are always anxious about everything. What He said was this. "Which of you by being anxious can add a single inch to the length of your days?" (author's paraphrase) Worry can't add anything to your life. It can't speed your growth. It can't make you stand an inch taller than you are. It can't pack an extra hour in the day for you to grow in. It can't give you any extra time to live.

Worry can't change anything that is truly important about your life.

So what *can?* If being anxious and dissatisfied about our progress in the Christian life won't speed up the maturing process, what will?

The Bible has a very basic answer. Growth depends on our daily relationship with Jesus.

The following chart shows what we've been saying so far in this chapter. Your new life has a goal and purpose; you are to be like Jesus. Throughout your time on earth, your destiny is to grow toward that goal. At any point in time along the growth line, you'll be able to look back (at past progress) and to look ahead (at more to be experienced and attained).

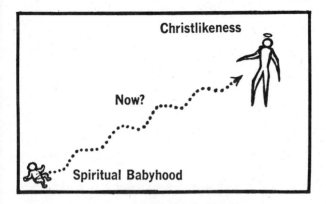

All life involves growth **over time** toward a goal . . . Christlikeness. At any given time, you will be **incomplete,** but accepted. Yet, what we do in our "now" has a great impact on the speed of our growth!

When you *do* pause to look back or look ahead, God wants you to realize that you are both incomplete . . . and yet fully accepted in Christ. He's not angry with you for not being fully matured yet. You are loved by your Father, and accepted by Him.

This growth line marks our passage through life over a period of time. It always involves looking ahead and looking back.

Earlier we noted that both *time* and *experience* count when it comes to maturity. But time doesn't automatically bring growth. And not every experience matures us. Growth comes from *time spent in reliance on Jesus;* the experience that helps is that of *living "in" Him.* What we are to concentrate on is not our past or our future. What we are to focus our attention on is being in fellowship with the Lord *now*.

John 15 is a well-known New Testament passage, one we need to consider to understand what we can do *now* to ensure growth toward maturity over the weeks and months and years.

John 15:1. Jesus begins by announcing to His disciples that He is "the true vine." The vine, on which grew the grapes so common to Palestine, is a much used Old Testament figure. Throughout the Old Testament *God's people* are presented as His vine, His "tender planting." God cultivated and nurtured His people, looking for them to bring forth fruit that would gladden His heart, even as the grapes gladdened the hearts of the Israelites. And what was the fruit he expected?

Righteousness! (see Isa. 5:1-7)

God has always wanted people who would be like Him: pure, loving, ever doing that which was right.

But God's Old Testament people failed to produce this fruit. Instead they offered bitter fruit to God: lovelessness, selfishness, exploitation, prejudice, discrimination, injustice. The taint of sin infected the fruit their lives produced, and that taste was bitter indeed.

But then Jesus came. And He announced, "*I* am the true Vine." I, not you, am the One who has the power to produce the fruit My Father has desired.

John 15:2. Then Jesus defined the relationship between us and Him. It is the branches which bear the fruit. But it is the vine, whose roots sink deep into the nourishing soil, that provides vitality and life to the branches. The fruit that appears in our lives can come only from Jesus' life-force. It is His fruit, made visible in us.

And God does intend that we bear fruit. He has the destiny of Christlikeness definitely in mind for us. Everything that happens to us—be it pruning or even painful times of loss of fellowship—is used by the Father to improve our capacity to demonstrate Jesus' life and bear Jesus' fruit.

John 15:3-6. Here Jesus makes clear that He is not talking about salvation, but fruitfulness. Don't fall into the mistake of thinking that God will cast you out as His child if He should seem to set you aside as a branch. He is speaking to those whose lives have been once and for all cleansed (15:3).

Yet He's warning us. A branch on an actual vine that doesn't bear fruit is cut off. Separated from the vine, it's useless. It dries up, and in a dried state the vines of Palestine are not even of use as firewood! Separated from the vine, a branch has no useful function. So you and I, separated from intimate interchange with Jesus, are useless. We dry up. In our dried state, we can have no useful function *as a branch*. We can never produce the fruit of Jesus' likeness, can never manifest His righteousness without Him.

So, Jesus instructs us, "Abide in Me." *The Living Bible* puts it well: "Stay close to Me." Stay close to Jesus, for when we are close to Him, His life flows through us and we begin to show His fruit.

It is on this "abiding" in Jesus that we are to concentrate. When we stay close to Him and draw on the power of His life, as a branch draws on the vine, then we grow. *It is time spent abiding in Jesus that is growing time for us.* The more time we spend close to Him, the more we mature, and the more we'll be able to say, "I'm growing."

John 15:7-10. Often to a new Christian, Bible terms such as "abiding in Christ" sound mystical and unreal. Too often for older believers these are merely familiar sounds, comfortable words, but words that have an elusive meaning hard to pin down and make practical. But normally such phrases are defined or made practical in the biblical context where they appear. It's that way here. Jesus explains in the simplest terms just what He means by "staying close to Him." Two elements are stressed:

Love. Strikingly, the love stressed in these verses is God's love for us! Jesus first affirms, "I have also loved you" (v. 9). God's love *is* ours. He has given it to us, and He will not change. But then Jesus says something strange. "I have also loved you; abide in My love."

Can we remove ourselves from God's love? Can we cut ourselves off from His concern?

When I was in seminary, my parents called to say that my father was to undergo an operation which he was unlikely to survive. It was major surgery, and his illness had wasted his once-sturdy frame to 140 pounds. I made plans at once to be with my mom and dad during the critical days. But after talking it over, they said, "No, don't come now. Come only after—if Dad shouldn't survive. Mom will need you much more then than now." And so while I waited in Dallas, Mom and Dad in Michigan faced the time of trial alone.

Did I love them? Yes, distance didn't change love. But distance did change the possibility of my love reaching them. I couldn't sit with my dad in his hospital room, just to be there. I couldn't wait through the long hours with Mom, perhaps just to hold her hand or share in prayer. Our separation left love unaffected, but the ability to express love was drastically impaired.

It's *this* that God cares about for us. It's not that wandering from fellowship with God will change His attitude toward us. No, you can always *know* that you are loved. But our wandering away from the Lord *can* keep us from experiencing the sense of His presence, and knowing the touch of His hand.

So it's important to grasp this truth. Jesus loves us as much as God the Father loves Him (John 15:9). And He wants us to stay close to Him so that we can experience the fullness of what that love can mean.

Response. The second theme in these verses is that of obedience, of responding when God speaks. We'll look more at this in the next section of this book, when we explore the behavior of the child of God. But for now, note that "keeping My commandments" is the *key to the abiding relationship.*

It's exciting to me that Jesus says, "Keep *My* commandments" (John 15:10). Sometimes we misread this as "Keep *the* commandments," thinking of the Old Testament Law written on stone and looming as a precipice which we are to try to climb. But Jesus said, "*My* commandments." And the same words as those recorded on stone, spoken by the loving voice of Jesus, sound very different. Jesus asks us to respond to *Him,* not to an impersonal standard of Law. And when we know His love, we're encouraged to step out and to obey. Surely He who loves us wants only the best for us, and His words will lead us in the best of ways.

So it isn't mystical at all, this "abiding." It's a daily choice to live Jesus' way and to obey Him in all that we do.

At this point, then, we can put several things together. *Growth* is a long-range thing, a gradual transformation of our character toward the likeness of Jesus. This growth process takes time, and it takes experience. But the key to growing is our daily choice to live close to Jesus *now*.

We can look back. But we can't relive our past.

We can look ahead. But the only thing we can do to enhance our future is to choose to follow Jesus now.

It's as we live in Him, abiding in Him and drawing life from Him as a branch draws on the vine, that our lives and our personalities are changed by His touch.

An Answer

So we see that there is an answer for everyone who feels discouraged about his growth as a Christian. First, don't expect too much too soon. Growth is a process that takes place over the years. Remember that right now, incomplete as you are, you're accepted.

Second, grab hold of what God has revealed about growth. He does have a destiny determined for you—to be Christlike, and to grow toward Him across the years. And, right now, you can take definite steps toward maturity. You don't do this by whipping yourself on to greater efforts or by shaming yourself into greater faithfulness. You grow by staying close to Jesus daily. Starting now.

Your life, and power for your life, is found only in Jesus.

You are a branch, and He is the vine. So stay close to Him. Count on His love, and when you hear His voice, obey.

GOING DEEPER

1. What's your life been like since you've been a Christian? Can you see growth? Where? Share with your friend(s) how Christ has begun to work His changes in you.

2. Often it's hard to accept ourselves as we are, knowing our incompleteness. How did you feel when you first read that we are to see ourselves as incomplete, but accepted?

   What in this chapter helps you understand why the author makes this statement?
3. The key to growing is relationship with God now. Without looking back in the chapter, write down the symbol Jesus used to picture our relationship with Him. What is the biblical reference for this teaching? Then compare your recollections with the text.
4. For memorizing this week: John 15:4-5 and Romans 8:28-29.
5. Bible study: Matthew 5:43-48; Isaiah 5:1-7; Galatians 5:22-23.

5 I'm Not Alone

Love, forgiveness, and self-acceptance are foundational building blocks for your Christian life. Yet, firmly grasping and holding on to the fact that you are loved, forgiven, and accepted, comes slowly for most people.

It took 20 years, and God's touch through some of her Christian brothers and sisters, for Audrey to realize these truths and apply them to her life. Here's her story, transcribed from a cassette tape she made after she shared her story with our Sunday School class:

"On January 22, 1973, I said, 'Lord, I quit.' I had come to the end of a long struggle. I had spent 20 years of my life trying to prove to God that I was worthy of His love. Most of my Christian life, I had fallen under the darts of Satan, who said, 'Audrey, you fail all the time. How you must disappoint God.' I had been a Christian for years but had never really felt accepted by Almighty God. And so I lived a defeated Christian life, always my own judge and jury.

"Eighteen months before this time we had gotten Chris, our second son, and he had cried ever since. Satan used this until I felt helpless as a mother. Satan continued working on me, telling me how I had failed God, how I was a lousy Christian, mother, wife, friend, and so on. Oh, how I thank God for my Christian husband, his patience and love, and for the prayers that were said for us month after month.

"One night we went to Chris' doctor to see how we should handle Chris. He sent me to a family counselor who had been a pastor. I went to the counselor on January 20th, and really poured my heart out. He spent 15 minutes listening to my frustration, not only as a mother, as a wife, as a friend, but mostly I guess I'd have to say as a Christian who wasn't growing. He looked at me and said, 'Audrey, get off the throne of your life. You are trying to be perfect, and you must stop, or you'll always be miserable.'

"The next day I went to church in rebellion, still fighting. A sister shared about being so sick she had prayed to die, and God had answered, 'First, you must want to live.'

"That next morning as I was mopping the floor, I said, 'Lord, I quit. I'm too tired to try to earn Your love any more.' And a new life began.

"God gave me 1 Corinthians 13:11. 'When I was a child I spoke and thought and reasoned as a child does. But when I became a man my thoughts grew far beyond those of my childhood, and now I have put away the childish things' (LB).

"I had acted like a child. Always poor me. Poor Audrey. Not really thinking of others. People had prayed that a child would stop crying, and God answered that prayer twofold. Chris and his mother *both* stopped crying.

"You see, I couldn't love anyone, until I first accepted the love of God."

Audrey had finally discovered that God doesn't ask for perfection. He asks only that we let Him love us.

Side by Side

The themes that we see in what Audrey says reflect what we've been exploring in the past three chapters . . . and add an important dimension. That added dimension is this: *God communicated His love to Audrey through others.* She wasn't alone in her reaching out to find God's way to live.

God used Audrey's husband—his patience and his love.

God used other members of her church, who prayed for her and Chris across the months.

God used the counselor, who forced her to face her hidden attitudes.

God used the sister who stood in church to share how God had pointed her to life.

Audrey was never alone. Always surrounding her was the warm support of God's other children.

That every Christian needs others is a lesson that was hard for Bill to learn. Bill was brought up to win—and to win he was sure he needed to go it alone. When he was 10, he was put off his little league team for two weeks for striking out with two men on base in the last inning. In the next 14 years of ball playing, Bill never struck out again!

Later, Bill learned another lesson. To be involved with other people makes one vulnerable to their mistakes. Bill dropped team sports and took up swimming. Since he was the only one involved, he could make sure he'd be the winner.

And win he did. In 103 meets, Bill lost only 3 times.

In college, Bill not only competed; he began to coach. His files contained the name and record of every swimmer in the state. He was always in the pool, or poring over his reports and records. Soon coaches across the state were calling this college student for help and advice.

Bill had mastered the way to win. Compete. Rely only on yourself. Insist on perfection. And—most important—go it alone.

Then Bill came to know Jesus, and God led him to seminary. He had never read the Bible before he went there. His wife (who had been securely on the shelf beside his swimming trophies) knew as little. The guy who always succeeded now seemed bound to fail. This was a new world. Others knew so much more. Finances were a growing problem. Studies often seemed so intellectual—and what Bill and his wife needed most was help to grow spiritually.

The old competitive way of life, the old pattern of trying to go it alone, didn't seem to work any more.

In November of their second year at seminary, God gave this young couple a second touch, a fresh burst of love. A retreat helped Bill to join with other Christians with the aim of helping each other grow spiritually. He discovered that in the spiritual realm it's not competition that counts—it's cooperation. No one can cope with life and win any prizes as a Christian alone. It takes team-work for the individual or the group to grow.

Bill was learning something that Audrey had discovered, something the Bible talks about at length. In fact, it's one of the main topics of the New Testament.

When God brings people to Himself, He also brings them *together*. He puts them together in His Church, which the New Testament often calls a *body*. And how exciting this simile is!

- Members of a body (hand and wrist, arm and torso) are truly close to each other. They're linked in the most intimate way.
- Members of a body need each other. A foot can't get along without the hand. Or the eye without the ear.
- The members of a body are subject to the same guidance. The head directs and coordinates the movements of the whole.

Gifts for One Another

First Corinthians 12 is a chapter of the New Testament that explores what we can, and are supposed to, mean to each other.

1 Corinthians 12:4-7. The passage focuses our attention on spiritual gifts, the special abilities God gives each Christian to help the growth of others (even as so many used their gifts to help Audrey). Paul, the writer of this New Testament book, points out that there are many such gifts—"varieties" in fact (v. 4). Perhaps there are more even than the Scriptures record. But each of these special abilities with which we enrich others' lives comes from the Holy Spirit. In each of us, it is God working to touch others (vv. 5-6).

One of the most exciting revelations here is that every Christian has been given such a "manifestation of the Spirit." And that it's been given for "the common good." Being with others in the *body* means that you not only receive but contribute as well! You're an important member of the family of

God, important to your brothers and your sisters because God intends to help and bless them through you.

1 Corinthians 12:8-11. This representative list of spiritual gifts provides a sample of ways we help one another. We may be used to speak a word of wisdom—as was Audrey's counselor. We may be used to heal hurt and rebellion, as was the sister who shared that God had invited her to live. We may be used to support and encourage faith, as was the church family that continued to pray for Audrey and Chris. We may be used in even more spectacular ways. But in every way, it is God the Holy Spirit who reaches out through our lives and personalities to touch and to comfort and to build.

Just how He will use you is up to Him to determine and to choose (v. 11). But you can know that He *will* use you. He has a special place and gift for you to use.

1 Corinthians 12:12-24. In these verses, Paul introduces the analogy of the body and points out that each member, no matter what his function, is important. Hand and foot, ear and eye, all are parts of the one body, and necessary to each other.

Sometimes a Christian wants desperately to be used by God, but thinks that the only way he can be used is to become a "full-time worker." He thinks of "ministry" as standing at a pulpit or as writing books. But God has a different perspective entirely! God places each of us in the body, designing us to fill a spot that no one else can fill. Here again Audrey's experience is helpful. *Not once* in her report does she mention her pastor. Or her Sunday School teacher. They certainly have had some impact on her life. But what God used to turn her life around was His touch through "common" people: her husband, a counselor, a sister who had known a similar despair. *It was these people who were God's gift to Audrey, and who in sharing with her were channels through whom God's love flowed.*

Isn't it good to know that you aren't alone? That God has given others to you—and you to others—that all might give and receive of His love?

"You are not alone" means that you need other Christians and they need you.

1 Corinthians 12:25-27. What kind of relationship with your brothers and sisters is necessary for you to be a part of this giving and receiving fellowship? We see it clearly here. There is to be no division in the body, but members are to have the same care for one another (v. 25). This doesn't mean that there can be no differences of opinion. Or that some of us may prefer to worship in special ways, or stress some doctrines rather that others. It does mean that our unity is to be expressed in *caring for each other anyway!*

This is one of the first things a new Christian needs to do: find a fellowship of Christians who really care about each other, and join them in loving and being loved.

There's an intimate relationship described in verse 26. Christians should be so close that we actually suffer with other members of the body, and rejoice with them. When we read of this kind of intimacy, we realize that being in the body means more than going to church or sitting in a pew. And more than shaking hands with acquaintances we see there. Being in the body means getting to know others well, sharing our hurts and joys with them, and opening our hearts to let them share with us.

And, because Jesus lives in each of His children, this kind of relationship is yours to know. As the

I'M NOT ALONE / 61

Bible says it, "Now you *are* Christ's body, and individually members of it" (1 Cor. 12:27).

That old competitive "go it alone" approach isn't for you. You stand, hand in hand, with a whole family of brothers and sisters that God has given you.

Deserted? Never!

Knowing that we have people to stand with us and support us is only part of our freedom from isolation.

We also have another Person with us, One who has promised, "I will never desert you, nor will I ever forsake you" (Heb. 13:5).

During the first days of her surrender to God, Audrey learned a lot about herself. "I asked God to show me who I was in those next few days," she says. "He showed me self-righteousness, self-centeredness, selfishness, and discontent. And I suddenly saw all those things as sin.

"I remembered Romans 3:23, 'For all have sinned and come short of the glory of God' (KJV). I knew then that I would fall short, all the time. And that this was the reason God had given His Son. So now I claim the blood of Jesus, accepting the love of God and the forgiveness of God. Now I do live a new life, learning, day by day."

But Audrey doesn't live this new life alone. Earlier we saw one of the special verses God gave her to help her understand herself. There was another passage, something God gave her to help her understand *Him*.

It was Matthew 11:28-30, "Come to Me and I will give you rest—all of you who work so hard beneath a heavy yoke. Wear My yoke—for it fits perfectly—and let Me teach you; for I am gentle and humble, and you shall find rest for your souls; for I give you only light burdens" (LB).

Audrey says, "I was a tired struggler, trying to do it all myself. You see, I found that in Jesus' time the mature ox wore a heavy yoke, and the younger ox walked by its side, with no weight on its yoke at all. The younger ox was simply being trained by the older animal. Jesus said, 'For I will give you only light burdens.' I found I could be like those little oxen if only I'd trust Jesus with my life: my present and my future."

It's a beatiful picture, and a true one: walking through life with Jesus at your side, turning your burdens and all of life, your present and your future over to Him, knowing that He will never leave you nor forsake you, and that as you trust Him, He'll take the weight of the load and live out His own life through you.

> All this is ours, God's gift to us in Jesus.
> We'll never walk alone.
> We have brothers and sisters.
> We have Jesus by our side.

GOING DEEPER

1. Do you think of yourself as more like Audrey "before" or "after"? Why?
2. Think of all the ways that God has used other people to touch and enrich your life. Jot down a list of those who have played a role and share this with your friend(s).
3. In this section of the book, we've looked at several basic truths about our attitudes toward ourselves, God, and others, attitudes that change as we come to know

God and His ways better. Check on the list below the truth you feel is most important *to you*. Share why this is important with your friend(s).

_____ I'm loved
_____ I'm forgiven
_____ I'm incomplete ... but accepted
_____ I'm not alone

4. For memorization and meditation, why not learn both Hebrews 10:24-25 and Hebrews 13:5?
5. Bible study: Romans 12:4-10; Ephesians 4:15-32.

PART II

NEW PATTERNS OF LIFE

As a Christian you'll develop new feelings about yourself and others. You'll find a freedom to accept yourself, and to love others even as Jesus does. There are also other new things to learn, other ways that God has made it possible for you to grow. You'll learn how to hear God's voice in Scripture, how to take difficulties and joys to God, how to share Christ with other believers and with your non-Christian friends.

Life will be different in the things you do—and want to do—as well as in the things you feel. In Christ you'll find new patterns of life that bring you abundant joy.

6 | Little Daily Steps of Obedience

When we met Ray in chapter one, he was living a defeated and unhappy life. Even though he'd been a Christian for a long time, and even though he was working full time with a Christian organization, Ray was overcome with discouragement. So much had gone wrong with his life. His dreams of a respected place in his organization and his hopes for a deep relationship with his family seemed doomed. His sense of inadequacy and, finally, of helplessness simply overwhelmed him.

Perhaps you've been a Christian for some time and found that life hasn't turned out any better for you than it seemed for Ray. If so, you can understand the depths of his depression. And if you're a new Christian, Ray's experience can warn you. Life doesn't *automatically* become new and exciting. God has marked out special ways for His children to grow. When we miss those ways, or turn aside from them, our life can be a downhill journey. But Ray found something out. *It wasn't too late for him.* God's ways to grow are open to us as soon as we begin our new life. Or growth can begin at that terrible moment when we face the fact that we've been missing out on life's meaning.

Weighed down and lost, Ray came to the end of his resources and turned his life over to God. And then Ray began the long climb back up by, as he puts it, determining to take little daily steps of obedience.

A Word from God

What Ray was talking about is one of the great resources God has given us for new life in Christ. Ray was speaking about the Bible, and his own response to it.

Sometimes we think of the Bible as a book of information about God. It is that. But the Bible is much, much more. When we understand that "much more," we can see how the Bible is to be used to enrich our lives and stimulate our growth in godliness.

Ray made a commitment to *put into practice* what he discovered daily in Scripture. He began to read daily, determined to rediscover how God wanted him to live.

Two nights ago I took my two youngest children fishing. We went out in our 12-foot boat, anchored along a shore as the sun was drifting down behind the Arizona cliffs, and waited for night. Soon it came, with a Western suddenness. And soon too the fish came, and the snags. All too often our hooks seemed to catch on the brush and rocks on the bottom, and all too often the only remedy was to break off the lines, fumble in the tackle box for new hooks, and rerig.

It was so frustrating, especially trying to tie hooks on the lines after dark. I had a fisherman's lantern.

At last I managed to hold the light between my knees, focus it on the plastic box that held my tackle, and see enough to tie my Crawford figure-eight knot. But I had to have that light focused on what I was trying to do to be able to see well enough to tie the knot.

The Bible uses a striking simile in speaking of itself, "Thy Word is a lamp to my feet, and a light to my path" (Ps. 119:105). Scripture isn't meant to be a sun that reveals everything in perfect clarity. It's meant to be a lamp, something we can focus to enable us to find our way with confidence. When God's Word is focused on what we're doing—just as my lantern was focused on that knot—we can know we're to live now.

It's this "lamp" function of the Bible that we need to apply in order to grow. It's true that the Bible does give the broad outlines of things as well. We can see it all in the pages of Scripture, just as I could see the larger features of the lake in the moonlight sitting in that boat. But I couldn't see every detail of those vistas. And I didn't need to! What I needed to see in detail was my hands, the fishline, and the knot I was trying to tie. *When I focused the lantern on what I was trying to do, I could see these things clearly.*

As I said, the Bible does give broad outlines of all things. These outlines are accurate, for God's Word is true. And we do want to know something of what God is doing in our world, of His plan for the future, and for mankind. But we make a mistake if we constantly focus our study of the Bible on these things. We need to focus the Word of God on what *we* are doing *now*. We need to focus Scripture on our present decisions, our present problems, our present needs. When in the light of God's Word we see clearly what we are to do, we need to commit ourselves to do it.

Using the Bible as a lamp for our *now* is the key to its contribution to our spiritual growth. It's for our growth that we've been given the Bible as a unique Word from God.

The Bible

This book that plays such a great role in our Christian life is unique. The books of other religions express man's search for God; the Bible expresses God's communication to man. Written over the span of at least a thousand years, by 40 human authors, the collection of 66 Old and New Testament books is marked by a fantastic unity, though God expressed Himself to us through very different men.

The process by which the Bible was given is called *inspiration,* a term that comes from 2 Timothy 3:16, which claims that "all Scripture is inspired [literally, *breathed out*] by God." The Holy Spirit, working through the distinctive personalities of each author, so moved them that the words recorded in the Scriptures are stamped as *God's* words (2 Peter 1:19-21). Over 2,000 times in the Old Testament alone the Bible writers declare, "Thus says the Lord"/"the Word of the Lord came, saying," etc.

Because of God's desire to communicate with us things we could never learn through experience alone (the very thoughts of God!), God revealed them through His Spirit (1 Cor. 2:9-10), and has given us His thoughts in words (1 Cor. 2:13).

Over the years, the words originally given by inspiration have been copied and recopied with such care that the Bibles we have today are essentially accurate and authoritative. When we pick up our

Bibles, we can be confident that God speaks to us, just as He spoke to the first generation of readers hundreds of years ago.*

Throughout the centuries, the Word of God has illuminated the lives of His children, communicating His love, giving life meaning and purpose. Man is far more that some chance assembly of atoms; he is the direct creation of God. And the Bible shows us how to live life at its best.

It's in all these things that we see our real need for the Bible.

Earlier we noted that one aspect of sin is inadequacy. We try, and fall short. We look, and can't quite see. This, the Bible says, is the state of all men, groping blindly for truth and for reality, but lost in a world of illusion as we follow this world's ideas of living (see Eph. 2:1; 4:17, PH).

Just a quick look around tells us how much man's ideas conflict and how uncertain our modern culture is. Men decry the immorality of war, yet defend sexual immorality in films and publications as free expression. Men condemn political corruption, but cheat on their taxes and find "little white lies" acceptable. Men say they want to show love, yet attack with hatred and violence those who disagree with them. What is right? What's wrong? What's helpful? What's a loving way to live with others? What is going to bring us and others happiness? The conflicting philosophies of men and the struggle to find meaning in so many different sources—in wealth, success, power, relationships, sex education, science —whatever, all testify graphically that we simply do not know how to live.

---

* For a brief study of what the Bible is and how to use it, see *What You Should Know About the Bible,* Larry Richards, Victor Books, Wheaton, Ill. 32 pp., 49¢.

Cutting across all the confusion, illuminating our world with light, has come the Word from God. He has shown us what is right and best. God has shown us how to live.

God's Word for Life Now

When Ray turned his life over to the Lord and determined to take those little daily steps of obedience, what he was saying was simply this: "I am going to seek guidance every day in the Bible, and *do* what God shows me." Scripture always connects *God's revelation and our response* of obedience.

Sometimes the word "obedience" brings up a rather grim picture. We visualize a sullen child or a slave, forced to do something against his will by a bitter and angry adult. The very idea of "command" conveys overtones of force and coercion, and an intense desire to be free.

But the Bible maintains a very different tone. It's the tone of a Person who speaks out strongly, but always in love. It's the tone of a Person who knows what's best, and who wants to warn us away from anything that might harm us and into a safe path. So in the Old Testament, God reminds His people through Moses, "The Lord commanded us to do all these statutes, to fear the Lord our God, for our good always, that He might preserve us alive, as it is this day" (Deut. 6:24, KJV). God's commands were given that we might *live*—and live abundantly. For that Word to enrich our lives and to "preserve us alive," we have to respond with obedience to the words He speaks.

The New Testament records an illustration used by Jesus to drive home the same point: God's commands are to be obeyed, not to avoid His anger but to assure a secure life. Jesus said, "Every one who hears these words of Mine, and acts upon them, may be compared to a wise man, who built his house upon the rock; and the rain descended, and the floods came, and the winds blew, and burst against that house; and yet it did not fall; for it had been founded upon the rock.

"And every one who hears these words of Mine, and does not act upon them, will be like a foolish man, who built his house upon the sand. And the rain descended, and the floods came, and the winds blew, and burst against that house; and it fell, and great was its fall" (Matt. 7:24-27).

In determining to begin to act on God's Word daily, Ray decided to stop living as a fool, and to become wise.

There are two passages of Scripture that help us put our relationship to the Bible in perspective. The first of these is in Hebrews, the second in John's Gospel.

Hebrews 3:7—4:11

In this passage the writer recalls an incident of Old Testament history well known to his readers, who were Hebrew Christians (as the title of the book indicates). The descendants of Abraham had been in Egypt for some 400 years, awaiting the time when God would keep promises He had made their forefathers about the possession of Palestine. When the time finally came, God acted in great power to free the Israelites from Egypt, where they had become slaves (Ex. 3—13). After freeing His people, God led them across a great desert to give them His commands, and then the people continued on to the Promised Land.

There, poised on the borders of Palestine, the Israelites hesitated. God spoke clearly to them, demanding they take the land He had promised. They heard what He said, but they refused to obey! They were afraid of the people living in the land, afraid that God would desert them, afraid to step out and appropriate the new life God had planned for them.

When they refused to act on God's command, God revealed to them the tragic consequences. They would be wanderers in the wilderness, knowing only the dusty and desolate places until that whole generation died and a new generation grew up that would follow God's leading. This is exactly what happened. The men and women who refused to act on the words God spoke to them never knew the blessings of the Promised Land. They lived and died in a desolate wilderness.

Now the writer of the Hebrews letter warns his readers. Watch out that the same thing doesn't happen to you. If you refuse to respond and obey when *you* hear God's voice *today,* then your life too will be a wilderness. You can only find rest by faith, the kind of faith that believes so firmly in God that it steps out to *act* on His Word.

Many of the thoughts of these chapters are vital for us.

Hebrews 3:12. We're warned against an "evil, unbelieving heart." Faith is trust ... and trust relies so firmly on Another that there is no hesitation in obeying.

Hebrews 3:18-19. God has uttered an oath: the disobedient will never know His rest. This isn't vindictiveness. It's simply a firm assertion that God knows the human heart. He knows how you and I must live to know peace and joy. God will point us to joy, but He will not manipulate reality to make us happy no matter what we do. If we disobey Him, we may be sure that we won't know the peace and rest that God has for His children.

Hebrews 4:7, 11. Here, too, the Word emphasizes *today*. "Today, if you hear His voice." The "rest" that Hebrews speaks of is not limited to the transfer of Israel from wilderness to the Promised Land. It's for us today too. We can leave the wilderness of spiritual dryness and defeat and know God's peace and joy *if we hear His voice and respond*.

And so the thought is summed up in verse 11. "Let us therefore be diligent to enter that rest, lest anyone fall through following the same example of disobedience." Let's watch out, lest, in coming to God's Word, we too fail to trust Him, and fail to obey.

John 14:15-24

We've seen something of the relationship between God's Word and obedience. In this passage Jesus made clear to His disciples another relationship—between obedience and love.

The Old Testament points out that God's commands are spoken for our benefit; His motive is clearly one of love. But love works both ways, for only love will move us to obey those commands.

John 14:15. Jesus introduces this theme by making a statement: "If you love Me, you will keep My commandments." Don't misunderstand this as an exhortation. It isn't saying, "You *ought* to love Me." Instead Jesus is making a statement of fact. He's saying that when we love Him, obedience does follow.

Sometimes, as we saw in another chapter, we feel that we "ought" to obey. We struggle on in futile self-effort to better ourselves. At best this falls far short of obedience. For obedience is not *compliance*—it's commitment. We who are parents might "make" our children do certain things by force or the threat of force. But we don't want them to comply sullenly, with rebellious hearts. We don't want them to do the things we tell them they should mechanically. Our goal is to help them choose what's right for themselves, to *want* to make that choice. Coercion may produce outward conformity, but love can produce persons who are committed freely to what is right.

This is what Jesus is saying. God doesn't want just outward compliance or a grudging decision to do something because we feel we have to. He only counts as "obedience" that which involves our hearts as well as our behavior. And the thing that moves our hearts is love.

When we love God, we *will* be obedient.

John 14:16. Even with love motivating us, we're unable to respond adequately. So to make obedience possible, Jesus has given us "another Helper," the Holy Spirit. This Person of the Godhead is with us, and stays with us always. We can count on Him to bring us out of the wilderness of our own inadequacy.

John 14:19. Then Jesus gave His disciples a special promise. After His resurrection and return to heaven, He would make Himself known to His brothers and sisters. *The Christian can actually experience the presence and the reality of Jesus.* This is something that is impossible for men who are not God's children. When we have this personal experience of Jesus as well as the objective truth of His Word, then we *know* that Jesus is God the Son—and that God is real.

John 14:21. Jesus then went on to promise that this self-disclosure would be experienced by all who have Jesus' commandments and keep them (that is, who love Him). When we hear and do God's Word as a love response to the Father, Jesus makes Himself known to us in a personal way.

John 14:22-24. This seemed a cloudy and mysterious statement to Jesus' disciples, who at that time had not even grasped the fact that Jesus would be crucified. So one of them asked, "How?" Jesus didn't explain how He would make Himself real to us. Instead He restated the critical principle. "If anyone loves Me, he will keep My Word; and My Father will love him, and We will come to him, and make Our abode with him" (v. 23). Love leads to obedience. And when a person obeys, living in the center of God's love, God is *there* in a special and experiential way.

This was what Ray experienced as he turned his life over to Jesus in commitment and began to take those daily steps of obedience. Each daily step brought more love for God, who had forgiven him in all his failures. And the freshened love for the Lord brought new impetus for daily obedience.

Today Ray *is* a different person than he was just eight months ago. He's moving out of his wilderness and into the rich, full life that Jesus promises. Ray is using the Bible as God intended, and its light is showing him the way.

GOING DEEPER

1. This chapter surveys several vitally important truths for our new life in Christ. The following list summarizes the main points. See if you can explain them

in your own words, and then check them out against the discussion in the chapter.
   - a. God's Word is to be focused on our daily life and decisions—on how to live now.
   - b. Guidance from God's Word is necessary because people do not know how to live well.
   - c. Knowing God's Word will not help us unless we respond in obedience.
   - d. God's commands are expressions of love, showing us the way to real life.
   - e. Faith in God and obedience are closely related, and disobedience is evidence that we do not trust God.
   - f. Love for God is the principal motivation for obedience. As we love Him, we keep His words.
   - g. We come to experience subjectively the reality of Jesus as we learn to live by the Word of God.
2. Talk over each of these points with your friend(s), thinking together about the approaches you've taken in reading or thinking about the Bible. If you have personally experienced some of these things listed above, share those experiences.
3. A simple "step by step" approach to Bible study might follow this pattern:
   - a. Read the Bible daily, asking God to show what you need to understand and to do *that day*.
   - b. When God does show you something, act on what He says.
   - c. If you feel hesitant or afraid, remem-

ber how much God loves you, and that He wants you to know the very best. Trust the Holy Spirit, your Helper, to give you the strength to obey.
4. A good passage to memorize this week is John 14:22-24
5. Bible study: Psalm 119; James 1:22-25.

7 | Leaving It with God

It upset Glenna to hear Bill and my wife speak of "committing the day" to God each morning, and that this simple action brought the day into perspective. She'd known so many ups and downs in her Christian life since her conversion. How could anyone promise God that *this* day would be His day? How presumptuous it sounded!

When Glenna shared her feelings with my wife, the situation became more clear. These members of our Tuesday night group had not been "promising God it would be His day," as if they guaranteed Him they would do no wrong. They were simply saying, "God, I'm leaving this day, and all that happens in it, to You. I trust You with it, and with myself."

This is something that the Apostle Paul talks about in Philippians. After encouraging us to rejoice in the Lord, who is near (4:5), Paul writes, "Be anxious for nothing, but in everything by prayer and supplication with thanksgiving let your requests be made known to God. And the peace of God, which surpasses all comprehension, shall guard your hearts and your minds in Christ Jesus" (4:6, 7).

Life, Paul is saying, isn't something to face with worry and doubt. Life is something to commit to God, letting Him know our needs and concerns, and then leaving it all with Him. When we learn to leave everything with God, then peace will guard our hearts and minds in every circumstance.

Dana

Dana knew that committing everything to God wouldn't take the difficulties out of life. She proved that on the high school retreat.

Yesterday, I preached at our church in Scottsdale. It's our practice to have open sharing at the service, as well as a time in the Word, and worship in song and testimony. During a brief period when our folks were greeting those around them in the pews, I heard 16-year-old Dana saying, "Praise the Lord." I leaned over and asked her why she was praising the Lord.

"Well," she told me, "it was the high school retreat last week. We were on a midnight hike, and I twisted my ankle, and they had to carry me back to camp. It was so embarrassing; all I could think of to say was, 'Praise the Lord.' "

"Tell him about the basketball," prodded the girl by her side.

"Well, we were playing," said Dana, "and I got hit in the side of the head. It knocked me right out, and afterward I was so dizzy I couldn't stand. They all thought I was concussed, and took me to the hospital, and I was so scared. All I could think of was, 'Praise the Lord.' "

"And she was sick all through camp," her friend prompted.

"Well," Dana went on, "I was sick every day. And a couple nights too. But the brothers and sisters really helped. And all I could think of was, 'Praise the Lord.'"

Dana at 16 has learned to leave everything with God, and even in embarrassment and in fright and in pain, she knew God's peace.

How do you react when things go wrong? How do you respond to disappointment? To pain? To public embarrassment? If these things and others like them throw you out of control, they don't have to. As a Christian now, you've been given gifts that you need only reach out faith's hand to take: the assurance that God is in charge of *that* day and *that* circumstance and the deep, inexplicable peace that leaving it all with God brings. Both of these gifts are received when we commit ourselves to the Lord, confident that His will is best for us and for others.

Sometimes God will allow difficulties to beset us. But even these will be for the best. God let Dana discover that Sunday morning how her troubles had blessed some of His other children. Later in the service, another of the teens got up and shared that she had spent a night up with Dana, as Dana's body had been wracked with the dry heaves. She'd been so impressed with Dana's constant praise of God. "I've been sick too," she told our congregation. "And I was able to praise God to myself. But I couldn't praise God aloud. It meant so much to me to see Dana praise God even while she suffered. It was a real encouragement to help me speak out in praise too."

Then Bob got up to share. "We decided that we'd better act on the Bible's instructions, so we went to Dana and prayed for her. And she got well, right away! In fact, the first words she said as she got right up were, 'I'm hungry!' She was sick again the next day, but we did see God answer our prayers when we trusted Him."

Dana's illness hadn't been pleasant. But it had been purposeful. God had given her His peace, and had taught and encouraged others through her experience and her praise.

We don't always find out right away what God's purposes are in our experiences. But we can be assured that there is a purpose in God's will for us. A purpose that is good.

When Glenna understood what committing one's day to God involved, she determined that she was going to do the same thing. Commitment—leaving it with God—was going to be her lifestyle too.

That first morning she faced a difficult decision. She had just moved to the Phoenix area, just found a new job, and now was looking for a place to live. She had decided she'd like a house trailer. We suggested that she see a Christian dealer who's a friend of ours, and when she did she found she could get a new trailer for less than the secondhand one she had almost purchased. That day she took off a couple hours from work, went to the trailer sales office, and had the fun of picking out her furniture and interior colors for her new home.

Then came the time to sign the papers. She pulled up a chair, poised the pen over the contract—and felt a strong surge of "wrongness." Somehow Glenna felt sure that God was speaking to her, directing her in this day that she'd committed to Him. So she apologized, explained that she felt sure God was leading her not to sign, and left.

She went back to work puzzled. Why? The price had been better than reasonable. The dealer was established, reputable, a warm and committed Christian. Why hadn't God wanted her to sign those papers? As she came into the office, her employer asked her in for a brief conference. And right then, she found out why. Her boss had decided to open another store and wanted to tell her that she would probably work out of that location. The new store was some 30 miles from the place where her trailer would have been! The move would come in January. She'd want to buy her trailer and arrange housing then, not now.

God's Will

Glenna, like Dana, was thrilled to know that God had really led her. And to discover why He had led in that particular way. Often we don't get such immediate insight into God's reasons. We may wait to see the why, or we may never know it. What we can know is that God has a special plan for each individual. *As you commit your days to Jesus, He will make that plan known and work out His will in you.*

In the previous chapter we saw that God has revealed His thoughts and purposes in the Bible. He's given us an accurate and trustworthy picture of past and present and future. He has also given us light to focus on *our* present, light to live by. These Bible principles express general truths for all His children. For instance, Scripture says we are always to act in love toward other people. Love is always God's will. And the Bible even goes on to tell us how we can show love. "Do not commit adultery," the Bible says, and lets us know that premarital and extramarital sex are *never* valid expressions of true love. "Lie not at all, but speak the truth with your neighbor" lets us know that telling lies, similarly, is not a way you can show love.

In speaking this way, the Bible records God's will for His children. It gives an objective revelation of right and wrong, telling us what God's will is.

But we also use the phrase "God's will" in a personal and subjective way. Used subjectively, "God's will" speaks of God's special plan for each individual. That special plan isn't in the Bible. Nowhere does the Bible say, "Glenna, don't buy that trailer." Nowhere does the Bible say, "When you're at camp in August, Dana, remember to praise Me."

The list of all the things the Bible does not say about God's will for us as individuals is endless. Does God want you to go back to college? To change jobs? Does God want you to marry now? This particular person? Or to wait? For how long? Does God want you to move? Does God intend for you to ride in this car pool, or that one? Is there someone the Lord wants you to speak with on the telephone today? Someone who may need help or encouragement? We could go on and on.

God cares about these details of our life, because He cares so deeply about us. He doesn't tell us how to meet them in the Bible, *but as we commit ourselves to Him, God will let us know His will for us individually*.

A couple months ago I spent a Sunday evening with a college-career group. I asked what they would like to discuss, what seemed most important to them right then. They all agreed that they wanted to discuss, "How can I know God's will for my life? How can I be sure about my decisions?"

Several shared that in making decisions they had simply "tried the doors." If the doors shut, they didn't try to go through. In this way, one college girl said, she had decided to go to Phoenix City College simply because, after sending applications to a half-dozen nearby schools, PCC was the first to accept her.

God can use circumstances to let us know His will. And He does. But this same girl shared a conflict she now faces. She has felt that she should transfer into a nurses training program. She applied to two schools, one on the east coast and one on the west. Both accepted her. Her fiancé will be moving near the west coast school. But her mother, who has cancer, will be near the east coast school. And there are other circumstances that push and pull her in each direction.

Finally, she said, she realized that she just could not tell God's will from the circumstances. So she had to ask *Him* to let her know where He wants her, personally. She had to look to God instead of circumstances, and commit her decision to Him. When she did, God gave her peace about one particular choice.

God promises, "I will guide thee with Mine eye" (Ps. 32:8, KJV). This is a beautiful picture of a person gazing into the face of the Lord for direction —so close to Him that he can look deep into the very pupil of His eye, and, by watching the eye, see which direction the Lord is looking. The next verse warns us not to be like the horse or mule that has to be goaded and prodded into the right path. What a contrast! God doesn't want to be outside our lives, standing behind us out of sight, pushing and prodding us by means of circumstances. God wants us to be close to Him, so close, looking to Him so intently, that we can sense and respond when He guides us with a glance.

This is why learning to commit our days to Jesus is so important. When we abandon anxiety and bring everything to God, our attention is focused on *Him*. Then, with our eyes on Him, He is free to guide us with His glance.

But how will we *know* that what we sense as direction really is God's will for us? The peace God gives, "which surpasses all comprehension, shall guard your hearts and your minds in Christ Jesus." It can't be explained. But, just as Glenna learned through the disquiet before she signed and the peace that followed, so will you *know*. If your life is committed to Jesus, He *will* direct you.

Is It Practical?

Much of what I've been saying probably sounds mystical and uncertain. In a way it should. The Bible does say that this peace "surpasses all comprehension." But there are principles that are very practical that flow from the Bible's teaching on this subject. Principles that have been illustrated over and over in the experience of Christians.

(1) Knowing God's will for your life starts with committing your life to Him. When you give each day to God, and in prayer bring all needs and decisions to Him, God commits Himself to guide you.

(2) God is a Person, and communicates personally. He can communicate through circumstances, through a friend, through a particular passage of the Bible. But remember that coming to know God's will is not a matter of pushing buttons. God isn't a computer. God is a *Person!* Because He is a Person, you can trust Him to let you know His will for you, and to make you sure.

(3) Sometimes you won't have assurance *before* you have to decide. Then you make the best

decision you can, remaining open to God and willing to make any changes He may direct. What's important here is an attitude of willingness to do God's will—no matter what it involves. So don't be upset if assurance follows, rather than precedes, some choices.

(4) Assurance that a particular decision is right is found chiefly in the form of peace. This is a subjective thing. But it is nevertheless very real. God does guard our hearts and minds from doubt and uncertainty by the gift of His peace.

So seeking to know and to do God's will for you isn't impractical mysticism. It's a very exciting dimension of your Christian life. It begins when you learn to commit your days to God consciously. It grows as you learn to leave even the things that trouble you with Him, at peace because He loves you so much.

Depending on God

Everything we've been thinking about in this chapter is closely related to a basic Bible theme. *We can depend on God.* We can trust Him with our futures and with our very lives.

The corollary to this is that we can't depend on ourselves. Glenna didn't know that morning when she looked at the trailer what the afternoon meeting with her boss would reveal. But God did! So Glenna needed to depend on God for guidance.

Dana was overcome with embarrassment and later with fear. She couldn't depend on herself to respond with courage or praise. But she could commit everything that happened to her to God. God can be trusted. And God even freed her to thank Him in her suffering.

Committing yourself to God and depending on Him frees you to attack each day with vigor and confidence. It's not *self*-confidence that's at the root of this victory attitude. It's confidence in God. The first nine verses of Psalm 37 are very rich, and help us to see what the attitudes of commitment and dependence involve.

Psalm 37:1-2. It's so easy for us to look at other people—people who don't know God—and be envious of their prosperity. They may be positively wicked, but they may seem to have life much easier than God's children. But these appearances are deceiving. Rather than fretting ourselves, or being overcome with envy and anxiety, we're to take an entirely different approach to life.

Psalm 37:3. This different approach begins with trust. "Trust in the Lord," the psalmist writes, "and do good." Our security will be found and experienced as we trust Him.

Psalm 37:4. "Delight yourself in the Lord" is a second aspect of this approach to life. Enjoy God! Be glad you know Him! And, the passage promises, "He will give you the desires of your heart."

This is a very special promise. God will not only see that you get what you want. He'll even work within your personality to help you *want* the things He has planned for you.

I have a son who loves pies and cakes. I often wish he'd want peas and spinach as passionately! There's nothing I can do about his desires, but God can and will do something about ours. Even things that seem like spinach to us now can become ice cream as we learn to love and enjoy the Lord.

Psalm 37:5. The invitation to "commit your way

to the Lord" also has an exciting promise attached. "Trust also in Him, and He will do it." It's this that frees us so completely. God has promised to *act* when we leave our problems to Him.

What a promise! How often have you or I longed for someone to take our burdens off our shoulders and bear them for us? Now God Himself holds out His hands to us, saying, "Commit it all to Me. Let Me take care of it; I will act!"

Psalm 37:7-9. Through contrast, these verses give us further insight into our new approach to living. We are to learn to be still and wait for God to act. Our frantic pacing of the floor, our anxious attempts to solve our problems are unnecessary and harmful. We can trust God. Even when it means waiting.

Waiting with confidence frees us from fretting ourselves and from anger (v. 8). Trusting all to God assures us that we will inherit the best, for it is the best He has planned for us.

If you've been the kind of person who is anxious, who gets upset with worry and breaks out in anger at others when you sense the uncertainties of life, what an exciting prospect God opens up to you.

No, God won't take anxiety all away permanently. But God has a gift for you—the gift of peace. As you act to commit your days to Him, bringing everything to Him in prayer and supplication, God will bring His peace into your life.

You'll know His will for you.

And you'll see Him act.

GOING DEEPER

1. What would you most like for God to take off your hands right now? Why not give it to Him? Read Psalm 37:1-9. Act

on each invitation given there, and count on each promise.
2. If you feel free to, share with your friend(s) what you've committed to the Lord. And over the coming weeks, share how God shows Himself to you.
3. If you have had experiences like those of Glenna or Dana, share these with your friend(s) too.
4. Psalm 37:3-5 is an exciting passage to memorize. So is Philippians 4:6-7.
5. Bible study: 2 Corinthians 12:1-10.

8 | Life's Overflow

Tom, the youngest Christian in our Tuesday night fellowship, recently introduced me to two people God used to bring him to Jesus. One was his cousin Mary, who had sat with him early one morning as he literally talked himself out of spiritism and to Christ. "I said something once in a while," Mary recalled, "but mostly I just sat there and prayed."

The other person was Mary's husband of one week, a guy who has been a Christian for only six months himself. "It was mostly his love," Tom recalls. "It was sort of like a long cable that held on to me, and drew me to God."

Possibly you've had this experience, introducing someone to the people God used to help you find Christ. Usually that's how it happens. Somebody tells you about Jesus. Somebody shares. Somebody shows you love and concern that is different. And a line is thrown out that leads to your rescue and your new life.

This is how the Good News spreads. From person to person. And, one of these days, God will use you to touch someone else and bring him to Jesus too.

Gotta Witness?

For some of us the idea of "witnessing" is rather frightening. We're not just sure what's involved. But soon after becoming a Christian we're likely to hear that we ought to get others to become Christians too. Perhaps we're given a "plan"—some three- or four-step sure-fire approach that we're to follow exactly. Perhaps we're told to go door to door and survey strangers, using the entrance gained to try to win their allegiance to the Saviour.

No doubt God has used such methods. But it's important not to confuse methods with the concept of "witness" seen in Scripture.

In the first place, the Gospel is really designed to be shared person to person. It's infectious—and just as contact is vital in spreading infection, the people you are most likely to infect with your love for Jesus are those closest to you. In the second place, what we are communicating is really *life*. It's the life we have in Jesus—a new life that frees us and changes us as persons—that will compel the conviction in others that this Jesus we talk about is real.

"Witness" then involves the visible expression of our life. It's this overflow of our new life that attracts and that gives us the opportunity to explain in words that Jesus is the source of our newness.

Understood this way, witness isn't something you have to do; *witness is who you are*. It's nearly always "who you are" that both creates the opportunity to tell others about Jesus and that validates what you say about Him. So when Jesus explained to His disciples, just before He was taken back to heaven to be with the Father, "You shall receive power when the Holy Spirit has come upon you; and you shall be My witnesses both in Jerusalem, and in all Judea and Samaria, and even to the remotest part of the earth" (Acts 1:8), He wasn't saying what they *ought to do* but what they *would become.*

The Holy Spirit, who now lives in you as He does in every Christian, both works within believers to change them and works through them and their words to bring faith to people with whom they share the message of Jesus. As He transforms you into the kind of person who reveals Jesus, and as He takes the words you speak and uses them to bring people to faith in Jesus, you become a witness.

Life's Witness

Sometimes this idea that we "witness" by who we are seems a little unreal. *How* does who we are witness? What is it about Christians that shows that Jesus is real? Scripture seems to point to two primary kinds of overflow.

Family love: Acts 4:32-34. People today, psychologists and sociologists tell us, are marked by an intense sense of loneliness. They struggle to find meaning in relationships. They reach out for something that has been lost in the uprooting of life that marks our society.

But it's always been like this. Even when people were forced into close association by the smallness of their communities, there was still a sense of loneliness. For loneliness is a result of alienation, a result of the barriers that build up between people as they hurt one another, find their desires frustrated, and seek to satisfy their desires by pushing others aside. So people have always been hungry for love and for acceptance. It's sin, not industrialization, that distorts and twists interpersonal relationships and brings an awareness of loneliness that nothing seems to overcome.

How jolting it must have been, then, to the people of Jerusalem to see a new community of love suddenly formed before their very eyes. As people responded to the message of Jesus, they stopped being isolated units, and became members of a close and loving family. We read, "And the congregation of those who believed [now numbering thousands!] were of one heart and soul; and not one of them claimed that anything belonging to him was his own, but all things were common property to them. And with great power the apostles were giving [verbal] witness to the resurrection of the Lord Jesus, and abundant grace was upon them all. For there was not a needy person among them, for all who were owners of lands or houses would sell them and bring the proceeds of the sales."

What's striking here is *not* any supposed comparison with communism. What is striking is that suddenly thousands of people *loved* each other! They loved with a visible commitment! Things (even the most important possessions) were unimportant to them. People who a short time before had been strangers were now loved. No wonder the apostles' witness was full of power! Every word they said about Jesus being alive was demonstrated in a thousand personalities. Nothing else but the resurrection power of God could explain the reality of the love manifested by Jesus' followers.

And this is exactly what Jesus said would happen.

In a key command, repeated throughout the New Testament, Jesus said, "Love one another. By this all men will know that you are My disciples, if you have love for one another" (John 13:34-35). A visible, Christlike love within the family of God is incontrovertible proof to the world that Jesus is real, and that those who love are His followers.

This is one aspect of witness. As you learn to love other Christians as Jesus commanded, and as the Holy Spirit enables, people who see this love expressed will "know" that Jesus is real. The overflow from your life will speak convincingly of Him.

Personality change: Galatians 5:22-23. Psychologists usually think of personality as the sum and interaction of the various traits (or tendencies to respond) that mark individuals. One person will meet a difficulty and tend to become despondent. Another, when faced with a difficulty, will plug on with dogged determination. Such different tendencies, all taken together, comprise personality, a complex of tendencies so great that each of us is a unique individual.

What happens to the personality when you become a Christian? At first, possibly very little. You still get upset. You still quit when a difficulty arises. But as you grow in your experience of Jesus' life, your attitudes and perspectives change. You find that your personality changes too. You begin to rejoice, even in the face of problems that once would have thrown you into despair. God is in charge; you've committed the problem to Him. His Spirit touches you, and you know a joy that others simply cannot understand. This too is part of the overflow.

The Bible says that the fruit produced by the Holy Spirit, who is working in your life now, is "love, joy, peace, patience, kindness, goodness, faithfulness, gentleness, self-control."

Recently a friend of mine went on an extended

vacation to her former home—and there faced crushing hurt at the hands of an old friend. As she shared with us, she told how amazed she'd been to listen to herself talk and to realize that somehow she was speaking in *love!* "I was really amazed," she said. "I thought later, *God, You must have really been helping me grow, because I could never have responded like that before!*"

Her old tendency to respond with anger or to retreat in pain has been replaced by something new, being built into her personality by God's Spirit. She felt peace. And she spoke in love. What a witness this was! What a tremendous evidence of the reality of Jesus Christ in her life! The new life of God had overflowed in an absolutely compelling way, and testified that Jesus is real.

So "witness" involves your life. It involves what God is doing in you and in me, and in our fellowship with other Christians. When the people who know us best see our lives, what we *are* is compelling testimony to Jesus.

Silent Witness?

Saying that Christian witness is bound up in the overflow of a life that Jesus is filling does not mean we rule out a spoken witness. In fact, it's going to take words to explain to others how Jesus frees us to live our new kind of life. It's going to take words to help them see that Jesus invites them to experience new life too. So we don't rule out words. What we do is *focus* our words. We remember that what is at issue in the verbal witness isn't arguing doctrine, or trying to make others agree with our interpretation of each verse of the Bible. What is at issue is life . . . and death.

People without Jesus are dead spiritually. They're lost in the very real guilt that sin brings, and they are under judgment. Yet Jesus has come and died for them, to give them life. So what we want to do is help others see Jesus as the One who offers them new life. A passage in 2 Corinthians helps us put it all in perspective (5:14-21).

2 Corinthians 5:14. "For the love of Christ controls us, having concluded this, that one died for all, therefore all died." This opening verse brings us face to face with basic issues. Jesus died for all. The implication is clear. Jesus had to die for all because all are dead! *All* desperately need the life He offers.

This includes the people we're nearest to, the people we brush up against every day. When we learn to look at them as dead, in need of life, we see them in a new way. How about your boss? Perhaps you've seen him as an authority, as a person to respect, or as someone who can reward or punish you. Have you seen him through the divine eyes, as one who is dead and in desperate need of life?

Seeing people as dead doesn't mean that we draw back from them or are repelled. Just the opposite. When we realize their need and see them as special to God, we're moved to reach out to them, just as Jesus reached out to us. It's Jesus' own love that begins to control us in our relationships with others. Reaching out to bring the gift of life because we care, is at the heart of our witness.

2 Corinthians 5:15. This verse continues the thought. Jesus died for all. Now that we have received life though His death, who are we going to live *for*? Paul's conclusion: let's live for Jesus. He gave up His life for us; let's return the gift, and live our life for Him.

Both these verses point out that love, and love alone, is capable of motivating witness. We love others—for Jesus does. Witness that is compelled by a sense of ought or obligation will always fall short of revealing the reality and love of Jesus. It takes love to communicate Him—because God *is* love.

2 Corinthians 5:16. Here Paul invites us to stop looking at people and categorizing them "according to the flesh." When we categorize people this way we feel awe for the president, contempt for the bum, respect for the important, and condescension for the young. Let's stop seeing people this way— and begin to see each person as a special, worthy object of our love. Let's see each one as dead or alive, and bear him the gift of life.

2 Corinthians 5:17. This is a verse we looked at earlier. "If any man is in Christ, He is a new creature; the old things passed away; behold, new things have come." Life has become new for us. Life will be new for everyone who comes to Jesus to seek new life in Him.

2 Corinthians 5:18. Paul now applies the earlier thoughts. All these gifts and this newness are from God, who reconciled us to Himself and brought us into harmony with Him through Christ. *And now God has given us this same ministry!* You and I have been given the privilege of presenting Jesus to others, and so to invite them back into harmony with God. Witness, then, is more than living the life. It is presenting Jesus, the Life-giver, to others.

Verse 19 points out that bringing men into harmony was something Christ accomplished potentially on the cross. But the "word of reconciliation"— that explanation of Jesus' great act of forgiveness— is ours to communicate. Your life's overflow can validate the words you speak about Jesus. It can give you many opportunities to talk about Him as people wonder about the change in you. But it can never be understood by others without verbal expression in "the word of reconciliation."

And this "word" *has* been committed to you. We are ambassadors, bringing the urgent message of peace to men who are at war with God and with themselves. How exciting that we can promise reconciliation with God, and offer the gift of His righteousness, as we tell our Good News (2 Cor. 5:20-21).

Simple Principles

What we've been saying about witness can be summed up in a general way and expressed in simple, practical principles. In general, let's realize that who we are and who we are becoming is critical in witness. As the life of Jesus overflows, it provides proof that He is real. This overflow will give us many opportunities to share with others about Jesus —and they need this verbal witness as well as to see overflow. They need it, because apart from Jesus they are spiritually dead, and it is word of what Jesus has done for them that calls them to life. This kind of witness, blending life and spoken word in a natural way, speaks powerfully to those who know you. And it is to these people, your friends, that God will use you to communicate His love.

What are some of the practical principles that come from our understanding of witness as overflow?

(1) Focus your attention on Jesus. Your effectiveness in witness depends on growing and being filled with Him.
(2) Don't wait till you're perfect to say some-

thing about the Lord. Your friends will observe the *process of change,* and this is far more compelling evidence of God's presence than is the end result! Don't worry about failing God or embarrassing Him. As I said earlier, you're incomplete, sure. But you're accepted. Even your failures will be used to show others that God is able to love you anyway—and that He can love them.

(3) Don't wait till you know everything about the Bible to talk about Jesus. It's *life* that is at issue, and what you experience is what you have to share. Keep digging in the Bible, certainly. But words of witness are to be focused on Jesus and on your experience with Him.

(4) Don't confuse "witness" with talking about your church or trying to get people to go there. It's not wrong to invite people to your church. But you don't want others to "join your religion"; you want them to know Jesus as Saviour and find life in Him. So talk about Him.

(5) You can use a "method" if it seems to help you, but don't rely on it. And don't think that it is the "only way" to point people to Christ. God's basic way to win people to Jesus is to show them Jesus in you, and let you point them to Jesus as you share His "word of reconciliation." Especially, then, don't confuse witnessing with buttonholing strangers. Witnessing focuses on the people you know and who know you.

(6) Reach out and get to know non-Christians. If you are a new Christian, you probably have non-Christian friends. Don't cut your-

self off from them. Christian separation doesn't involve breaking off relationships, although some have perverted it to mean that. God loves non-Christians. Feel free to love them too.

Let God use you as He wants, not feeling forced by obligation to convince other people to believe in Jesus, but opening your heart to God, to let Him transform you and give you concern for your friends. Without strain, without the push of guilt or "ought," let Jesus fill up your life until it overflows. In the overflow you'll bring to others around you the water of life.

GOING DEEPER

1. How were you introduced to Jesus? Relate your experience to your friend(s).
2. The author has included a list of six practical principles on pages 98-100. Would you want to add to this list? Or change anything about it? Discuss.
3. How has the thought of "witness" made you feel in the past? Write down your feelings and then read over the chapter. Beside each recorded feeling, jot down ideas that tend to confirm or modify it. (For instance, if you've thought that witnessing was telling someone how to become a Christian and pressing for a decision right then, what impact does this chapter have?)
4. For memorizing: Acts 1:8 and 2 Corinthians 5:14-15 or 20-21.
5. Bible study: Acts 3—4.

9 | Growing Together

Because we had some newcomers in our Tuesday night group two weeks ago, we took time before our study to introduce ourselves. Person after person of the 25 or so in Bill's living room shared how "the group" had helped them grow. One or two, who'd been Christians for some time, said that only since they'd joined us could they see personal spiritual growth in themselves.

I was a little upset—and said so when my turn came. I was upset because we sounded as though there were some power in "the group" to change men, while our transformation was actually from Christ. I didn't want anyone to look to *us* to help him but to look only to Jesus. Still, I knew what they meant. Jesus was touching us *through each other*.

So far we've seen three ways to grow as Christians, three important ways of life that are important in building our new life in Christ.

- We need to be people who look into the Word of God and respond to what the Lord says to us with little daily steps of obedience.

102 / BORN TO GROW

- We need to be people who trust everything in life to God, and commit everything to Him in prayer and supplication—with thanksgiving.
- We need to be people who show the mark of Jesus on our lives and characters, and, out of the overflow of lives He is filling up, to share the Good News of His love and reconciliation.

There's a fourth critical factor in growing that we need to consider now. You and I need to be people who don't try to go it alone We need to build intimacy with other Christians, so that we can grow together.

Reach Out

We saw in chapter 5 that when you and I became Christians, the Holy Spirit joined us to Christ *and to each other*. We saw too that God fits each of us into this body in a special way, by giving us special abilities to help others grow. The Bible calls these special abilities "spiritual gifts." Through relationships with other Christians, God can use these gifts to help each of us grow. In fact, the Bible makes it clear that it's only "by that which every joint [part] supplies, according to the proper working of each individual part," that the body builds itself up in love (Eph. 4:16). When you and I are exercising our proper function in the body, each of us is going to grow steadily toward maturity in Christ (Eph. 4:13).

What, then, is "working order" for the body? How does this building up and maturing process happen? Scripture's answer to these questions is clear and simple: you and I are in "working order" when we have the relationship with other believers that God intends. *Personal relationships among*

Christians are the key to body growth and to the use of our spiritual gifts.

Love. The critical word in the New Testament about relationships between brothers and sisters in Christ is love. On the night before He was crucified, Jesus gave His disciples careful instructions about the future. Our record of that discussion contains in seed most major teachings of the New Testament. He began His teaching at this point: "A new commandment I give to you, that you love one another, even as I have loved you, that you also love one another. By this all men will know that you are My disciples, if you have love for one another" (John 13:34-35).

Over and over from this point on, the New Testament stresses love within the body. "Love does no wrong to a neighbor," Romans reminds us; "love therefore is the fulfillment of the law" (Rom. 13:10). But love is more than not doing wrong. Love is an active, positive reaching out. Love links us together in a bond of unity (Col. 3:14). Love is the goal of the teaching of God's Word (1 Tim. 1:5). We are to "love one another, fervently and from the heart" (1 Peter 1:22, PH).

I was in the Navy, stationed in Brooklyn, N.Y., when I met my wife. She lived in Brooklyn too, but about 20 miles away from 58th Street and 1st Avenue where I was. Still, every evening I found a way to leave the base and go out with her. At night, after our dates, we'd sit in my car and talk until very late —so late that those 20 mile drives home were especially tough. Yet, night after night, I'd snatch my few hours sleep, work through the next day, and dash out in the evening to be with her again.

This is something that always seems to mark love. When you love someone, you want to be with her.

Never make the mistake of thinking that superficial friendships are the fulfillment of Jesus' command to love each other. Or that having coffee or serving on a church board together is fellowship. Love is a lot more than this.

Love involves intimacy, and the desire to be with those we care for.

One another. Two phrases always impress me in Jesus' original command to love. We're to love "as I have loved you," and we're to love "one another." The first phrase tells me that the love Jesus is thinking of is a reaching out, initiating kind of love.

Jesus didn't love us long distance. He saw our need, and hurried to meet it. He came into our world, reached out to us, and met that need. Sometimes you and I may feel a need to be loved. How often do we sit back, and wait for someone to take the first step? When no one reaches out to us, we're deeply hurt, and wonder, "Where is this love we've heard of? Why isn't there more love in *my* church?" But when we look at Jesus' example, we find that He didn't sit back and wait, or criticize people for not loving Him. Instead, He took the initiative. Jesus' kind of love reaches out to people *first*. So reaching out is something that He expects from us. We're to reach out to others who may be uncertain, or frightened, or indifferent, and thus unable to reach out to us.

The reason the phrase "one another" excites me is that, as I look through the New Testament, I find it occurring over and over again. And wherever it occurs, it defines in a practical and operational way just *how* love reaches out.

Looking at "one another" passages, we see that love means getting close enough to each other to hurt and be hurt, for we are to be "forgiving each other, whoever has a complaint against any one; just as the Lord forgave you, so also should you" (Col. 3:13). We're to "accept the one who is weak in faith" (Rom. 14:1). Accept means welcome into close fellowship, as in Romans 15:7, where we're told to "accept one another, just as Christ also accepted us to the glory of God." God has welcomed our brothers and sisters into His family; how can we hold them off at arm's length?

We could go on and on. "Bear one another's burdens" (Gal. 6:2). If you're hurting, share it with a Christian brother or sister. If they are hurting, or in need, listen in love, and do all you can to shoulder the problem with them. "Stimulate one another to love and good deeds" (Heb. 10:24). Don't let another believer be alone, but encourage him to live Jesus' way.

Wherever we look at "one another" we find people that love has linked together in intimacy, people who truly care for each other and share their lives in meaningful ways. The Christian is a person who doesn't have to go it alone any more. As a Christian, you are part of a family where people really care.

Your Church

The need for fellowship is one of the basic reasons why Christians need to be part of a local church. The Church (capital C) is the body of Christ. It's comprised of everyone, past and present and future, who has come to know the Saviour. This Church is worldwide. You and I have brothers and sisters in Russia and China, in Germany and Brazil and Argentina, in Vietnam, in Boston offices and New Mexico communes. What links us to all these people is Jesus, and the fact that the Holy Spirit has joined us to Him and to each other.* You also have brothers and sisters in Christ right there where you live. And you ought to meet with them—to begin to experience the kind of fellowship we've been seeing in this chapter.

Normally, Christians group themselves together for worship and teaching and fellowship in a local church—an assembly of some of the Christians in a locality. Often there will be more than one church where people who know and love Jesus meet. It's important that you join with one—the one God leads you to. This is important for your growth as a Christian, and for the growth of the body.

Sometimes, though, your local church may seem something of a disappointment. Particularly if you are eager for the kind of "together" relationship we've seen the Bible describe. You may find that while the people in your church are friendly, they are not ready for intimacy.

But don't expect every church to be living up to the biblical ideal. In fact, don't expect *any* church to be! You and I are incomplete, remember? In just the same way, fellowships of Christians are incomplete too. But, though we've all got a long way to go, let's not forget that we are accepted.

Actually, this is why you're needed. The growth of the local church depends on what each believer in the locality can contribute. So don't make the mistake of some who get discouraged and abandon their brothers and sisters in the local churches. Remember that Jesus' kind of love initiates. If you're not satisfied, don't wait for others to take the first step. Reach out to them with a Jesus-kind of love.

---

* For a study of the nature of the Church and how we can experience our unity in Christ, see *Becoming One in the Spirit,* Larry Richards, Victor Books, Wheaton, Ill. $1.50.

Today, God is moving in exciting ways to revitalize the "together" life of Christians. Some churches, like the one I attend, have small groups that meet week nights for a more intimate sharing and study than is possible when a hundred or a thousand people are gathered.* Others encourage members to find partners who will pray with them and with whom they can share. In many more, sharing is encouraged during church services that once were formal and marked by a "one way" communication from the pulpit.

The most important thing for you, though, is to reach out to others. Invite them into your life, and get to know and care about them. Share what God is teaching you from His Word, and what you're experiencing of Jesus. Share what is troubling you too, and learn to pray for each other. Now that you are freed to love, as the Bible says, "love one another fervently, from the heart."

In reaching out, in loving, you'll discover that God has given others to you—to help you grow.

Approaching Life Together

The Bible presents love as the key to our life with other believers. But there's also an attitudinal key: an attitude toward each other that we need to develop. This attitude is laid out in Philippians 2:1-13, where Paul explains how we can be "with one mind striving together for the faith of the Gospel" (1:27).

Philippians 2:1. Paul begins with a statement of those things that motivate a love-produced unity. He speaks of "encouragement in Christ." Thank God,

---

* For an explanation of what happens in such small groups, see the author's book, *69 Ways to Start a Study Group and Keep It Growing* (Zondervan, Grand Rapids, Mich., $1.25).

there *is* encouragement. We are not doomed to be forever what we are now, but growth and change are certain. He speaks of the "incentive of love." It really is love that moves us. He speaks of "fellowship of the Spirit." How exciting that we all, as believers, do participate in the Holy Spirit, who links us as one in Christ. Each of these relationships is real. And the affection and compassion that flow from our relationship with Jesus are central in our attitudes toward each other.

We are to look at each other as brothers who are eternally linked in the Lord.

Philippians 2:2. Because of the relationships that do exist and what they mean to us (encouragement, incentive, fellowship), we are to work toward an experience of unity.

We are to be "of the same mind." This does not mean that we have to agree with each other on every detail of doctrine and practice. It does mean that we have the same "mind set." That we view each other in just the way verse one describes— as people who may be different but who are still in one family.

We are to have the "same love." When we maintain an attitude of acceptance toward each other and reach out to each other to find Christ's kind of intimacy, we will find that we *are* "united in spirit."

United, then, we are able to be "intent on one purpose." What is that purpose? I think it's to find and do God's will for us, individually and corporately. For Jesus is head of the body of which we are members. Our purpose is to accomplish His purpose in us and through us.

We may sometimes disagree with each other on how to accomplish that purpose. But disagreement over methods should never be allowed to disrupt unity. What really counts is that we have the same purpose and goal.

It's been exciting to see this principle work out. Our Tuesday group started with six people, three couples who were close in background and theological perspective. But soon the Lord added many others. Now we range in age from teens through 50s. People who do not attend our church come; we now include four Catholics, two Jewish Christians, Anglicans, Baptists, and I'm not sure what else. A couple members of our little group are charismatics. The youngest Christian has been saved for just two months now, the oldest for well over 30 years. Educationally we range from high school graduates through the Ph.D. Our jobs vary too: newspaper proofreader, secretaries, salesmen, a doctor, a swimming instructor. *Yet with all our differences, we know a unique unity.* We have come to love each other, and we're intent on one purpose: joining together in searching God's Word to come to know and do His will. And the non-Christians who frequently visit us have been impressed with the reality of Jesus Christ.

Philippians 2:3-4. For us to experience this kind of unity we need to approach living together with certain commitments.

Don't act from selfishness. Christian fellowship is not just for what we can get out of it. It's for what we can get *and give*. When we make each other the center of our concern, then all of us grow.

Don't act from conceit. Sometimes our chief concern is that others recognize our superiorities. Or that we get recognition. Or that we be the "leader." Life in Christ means cooperation not competition. Jesus is to be the center of our attention, not you or me.

Be humble enough to see others as important.
We've found that each person in our small group makes a distinct contribution to the whole. Looking at others as "more important" means recognizing and valuing what they contribute. Valuing them even more highly than we do our own contributions. It's exciting to find the freedom to be delighted when God acts through someone else, with no need to be jealous that He's not doing it through us. Looking at others as "more important" doesn't mean that they *are* more important, for the Bible says that *each of us* is necessary to the others. But we are to get our eyes off ourselves, and look for things to appreciate in others.

Don't look out for your own interests only. It's not that our interests are not important. They are. It's just that they're not to dominate our thinking. We're to learn to let others share the focus of attention. How good it was of God to give us others to care for. And how much lighter a burden seems when we know others care for us.

Philippians 2:5-8. If this way of life that the Bible calls "humbling" seems difficult, we can know that Jesus has passed this way before us. For Him to empty Himself, and set aside His prerogatives as God, was far more costly than any surrender of our "rights." For Jesus, giving Himself was total and extreme. He became a human being ("form" here does not speak of outward appearances, as of jello poured in a mold, but of complete identity). He became a human being who lived without even the status of human authority, and who ultimately suffered a criminal's painful death.

Jesus knew by experience just what this removal of self from the center of one's life involves. And Jesus knows the results!

Philippians 2:9-11. The result of self-humbling for Jesus was exaltation. God the Father brought His Son back to His rightful place by the Father's side. And gave Him the name *Lord*. Every knee will bow to Jesus, and every tongue one day will confess that Jesus Christ *is* Lord.

Many passages tell us that Jesus' death meant life for us. How good to realize that for Him also the cross was the doorway to even greater glory.

Actually, it's the same for you and me. Living this Jesus kind of life with each other, humbling ourselves for love's sake, is our doorway to glory too. As we live this way, together, God the Holy Spirit touches us and works in us His transformation. It is this becoming more and more like Jesus that is our glory and our goal.

Philippians 2:12-13. This kind of life isn't held out to us as easy. It is presented realistically as a life of obedience filled with difficulties that we are to face with "fear and trembling." But we can know, as we hold fast to Jesus' attitude toward others, that we will work out our own solutions (for this is the meaning of "salvation" here). We will work it all out because God is at work in us. And it's God, at work in our lives, who is able to accomplish His good purposes, even in you, and even in me.

GOING DEEPER

1. If you have been studying this book with others, perhaps you have begun to develop the kind of relationship that this chapter describes. On the line below, mark where you feel you are in your progress toward an intimate, love relationship with your friend(s).

```
|1    |    |    |    |    |    |    |
```
VERY SUPERFICIAL   DEEP LOVE

2. Share with your friend(s) how you marked the line above and tell why. Talk together about how you can move further toward Christian love's fullness —together.
3. In a concordance, look up "one another" references in the New Testament. See what else you can discover about how Christian love works out in practice.
4. For memorizing this week: Philippians 2:1-8. This is a long passage, but a rich one on which to meditate.
5. Bible study: 1 Corinthians 13; Romans 12:1—15:5.

PART III

NEW AWARENESS OF GOD

Being a Christian involves more than the discovery of a new self and of new ways of life. Being a Christian means discovering more and more about the Person who loves us and has welcomed us into His family. God the Father, God the Son, and God the Holy Spirit, now touch our lives in new ways. And we respond to our God, building our lives on who He is and how He acts. Our whole perception of life changes and re-forms—around Him.

10 God, Our Father

Marti grew up in a home dominated by her mother. She felt intensely her mother's coldness and brutal unconcern for her childhood hurts and pains—an unconcern that seemed to worsen as Marti passed into adolescence. Teach Marti to cook? "Get out of the kitchen! You're too clumsy and slow. I can do it easier myself."

All the time she was growing up Marti felt that her dad, at least, loved her. Sometimes he even took the family to the beach, or to visit the zoo. But, like the children, dad was dominated by mother. He loved Marti, but he never took her side. He loved her, but he loved her ineffectually.

No wonder when Marti became a Christian she had a hard time trusting God. The Bible pictures God as a heavenly Father, and whenever Marti thought of Him, the vision of her loving but weak dad seemed to intervene. She saw God as a carbon copy of her earthly father, and she just could not bring herself to trust Him.

This same thing happens to many of us. Our

father image is shaped by experience with our own family. Emotionally, if not intellectually, we perceive God as like our parents. Not that this is bad or wrong. In fact, God established families, in which parents are to model who He is. But it's the good father, not the bad or weak, who reveals the character of God.

Why does God present Himself as our Father? Because God wants us to take our place as His children. God wants us to grow in a relationship with Him in which we learn to depend on Him, even as our little ones depend on us. Such dependence is a healthy and good thing—a thing designed to help us grow.

Something to Grow On

Sometimes people doubt that dependence encourages growth. Many kinds do not. We've all heard stories of sick parents who try desperately to keep their children weak and dependent. A mother may insist on dressing a five-year-old in baby clothes. A dad may not let young teens cross the street without him. These parents aren't concerned with helping their children on to maturity (which is what God planned the family to foster). These parents seem concerned only about themselves and their own need to have someone remain forever weak so they can pretend to be strong.

But the right kind of dependence does not foster weakness; it fosters strength.

Our daughter dropped a soft drink bottle on the drive the other day, then stepped on a piece of glass, driving it into her heel. She stumbled to the front door, rang the bell, and sat down in a pool of blood to cry. We came. Tim, our youngest, was really upset at the blood; he dashed off in panic to get towels. Paul settled down beside Joy, found the wound, washed it, and removed the fragment of glass. All the while he talked calmingly, mixing sympathy and stability, bringing her the physical help she needed and setting an example of calm that quieted her fears.

How much Joy needed someone to act as a parent for her just then! Someone to meet the need, and at the same time teach her by example how to respond to sudden pain and fear. Joy was dependent on Paul during those moments, in the best sense. She looked to him for help and for guidance. In her dependence, she received help *and grew.*

Life so often pierces our heels. To whom do we turn? Where do we go for help? Where do we go for the calm we need and the stability? The Bible tells us that we can depend on God at these times, that we are to "come boldly unto the throne of grace, that we may obtain mercy, and find grace to help in time of need" (Heb. 4:16, KJV). Like little children, we are to turn immediately to our Father, deeply aware of our limitations, depending on Him for help and for grace to grow.

I mentioned in an earlier chapter that Tim wanted a telescope. He studied telescopes, found that he'd need a refractor scope with an equatorial mount, and then came to me about the money. Tim had some money saved, but it wasn't enough. He needed more, and he had no way to get it. Who else could he turn to? Who else would care? (Certainly not the neighbors. A child can't approach them with financial need!) His mother and I talked it over, and talked with him. We could have simply given him the money. But that wouldn't have helped him grow. So we worked out a way by which he could earn what was needed—part before the purchase and part after, for he wanted it soon to use during the summer nights when he could stay up late.

Tim came to us because he depended on us to meet his needs and satisfy his wants. And we used that dependence to help him grow in responsibility and self-reliance. Dependency became an opportunity to help Tim grow.

This is what dependence on God involves for us. It's not that God wants to keep us weak. As a Father, God wants us to depend on Him in order that He might guide us toward maturity in Christ. Recognizing our total dependence on God for all things fits the fact that we *are* dependent—and it's a critical ingredient in becoming Christlike.

This, of course, is what Hebrews 12 is saying. God speaks of human fathers who "disciplined us for a short time as seemed best to them, but He disciplines us for our good, that we may share His holiness" (v. 10). When we receive Christ, God receives us as His children; now He wants to act as our Father. He invites us to depend on Him *completely,* and promises us that this dependence will help us grow.

Love and Power

It's hard to have an attitude of dependence on God if we've had parents like Marti's. Somehow, even if we're sure God loves us, we can't help seeing Him as weak and impotent and unable to intervene. Others have known a strong father—one who was powerful, but unloving! Probably these are the two most common distortions of our concept of God's Fatherhood. We may feel He cares, but be unable to trust Him because he doesn't seem to us to be in full control. Or we may be so awed by a sense of His overwhelming power that we cringe back, unable to believe He could love us.

Yet the Bible presents God to us as both all-loving and all-powerful. Seeing Him this way, as He is, enables us to live in proper dependence.

Love. Through Luke (11:1-13), God calls our attention to His love. The passage begins (vv. 1-4) with a prayer that Jesus taught His disciples; a prayer that begins by recognizing God as Father and moves on to ask Him for all things: direction (His will), sustenance (daily bread), forgiveness, guidance, and deliverance. In this prayer, Jesus calls our attention to the fact that life is not "doing something for God," but rather living in awareness that God delights in doing things for us.

Jesus then (vv. 5-10) tries to teach His disciples by contrast. He brings out false concepts of God to show how empty they are compared to the reality. He tells of a man who has an unexpected visitor, and who goes to a neighbor to ask for a snack to give the late arrival. From inside the neighbor shouts, "Don't bother me!" Jesus' commentary? If the man simply keeps on pounding, the neighbor will finally get up and give him the food just to get rid of him. And Jesus' point? *God is not like an uncaring neighbor.* God doesn't treat us like strangers who are bothering Him.

Jesus tells us to address God as "Father," not as "friend." And so He goes on to promise, "I say to you, ask, and it shall be given to you; seek, and you shall find; knock, and it shall be opened to you." The Father is eager to meet needs while a friend might only supply to avoid unpleasantness.

God not only invites us to come to Him; God promises to respond.

The next verses (vv. 11-13) tell us more about that response. "Now suppose," Jesus continues, "one of you fathers is asked by his son for a fish; he will not give him a snake instead of a fish, will he? Or if he is asked for an egg, he will not give him a scorpion, will he? If you then, being evil, know how to give good gifts to your children, how much more shall your heavenly Father give the Holy Spirit to those who ask Him [or, 'give good gifts to those who ask Him']?"

God will never be angry with you for asking!

God will never play tricks on you, or give you anything to hurt you when you ask for something good. Even human parents, tainted as we all are by sin, don't act this way with our children! How could we ever imagine that God, who is perfectly good and completely loving, would ever give us less than His best? And, with all the good He gives us, God has given us Himself in the Person of the Holy Spirit.

No, when the Bible presents God as "Father," Scripture asserts the uniqueness of His love for you, His child.

You can bring every need and desire to Him.

You can be sure He is listening, willingly.

You can be sure He'll answer.

You can be sure His answer will be good.

This is God's love-commitment to you. This is what it means for Him to affirm that He is your heavenly Father. His attitude toward you will never change. You're in His family now, and you can depend on His love.

Power. It's important to realize that this fatherly love-commitment is made by *God*. God's people have a habit of forgetting who He really is. So God has reminded us—by acts of power, by miracle, by words. Some of these words are so rich that we need to read them over and over to sense, with awe, just how great God really is. Listen to these, from Isaiah 40.

> Who has measured the waters in the hollow of His hand,
> And marked off the heavens by the span,
> And calculated the dust of the earth by the measure,
> And weighed the mountains in a balance,
> And the hills in a pair of scales?
>
> Who has directed the Spirit of the Lord,
> Or as His counselor has informed Him?
> With whom did He consult and who gave Him understanding?
> And who taught Him in the path of justice and taught Him knowledge,
> And informed Him of the way of understanding?
>
> Behold, the nations are like a drop from a bucket,
> And are regarded as a speck of dust on the scales;
> Behold, He lifts up the islands like fine dust.
> Even Lebanon is not enough to burn,
> Nor its beasts enough for a burnt offering.
> All the nations are as nothing before Him,
> They are regarded by Him as less than nothing and meaningless. *(vv. 12-17)*
>
> Do you not know? Have you not heard?
> Has it not been declared to you from the beginning?
> Have you not understood from the foundations of the earth?
> It is He who sits above the vault of the earth,
> And its inhabitants are like grasshoppers,
> Who stretches out the heavens like a curtain
> And spreads them out like a tent to dwell in.

> He it is who reduces rulers to nothing,
> Who makes the judges of the earth meaningless.
> Scarcely have they been planted,
> Scarcely have they been sown,
> Scarcely has their stock taken root in the earth,
> But He merely blows on them, and they wither.
> And the storm carries them away like stubble.
>
> "To whom then will you liken Me
> That I should be his equal?" says the Holy One.
> Lift up your eyes on high
> And see who has created these stars,
> The One who leads forth their host by number:
> He calls them all by name;
> Because of the greatness of His might and the strength of His power
> Not one of them is missing. *(vv. 21-26)*

And yet, this God of almighty power bends not only to notice us but to give of His strength to us when we grow weary and fail. For the same passage continues:

> Do you not know? Have you not heard?
> The everlasting God, the Lord, the Creator of the ends of the earth
> Does not become weary or tired.
> His understanding is inscrutable.
> He gives His strength to the weary,
> And to him who lacks might He increases power.
>
> Though youths grow weary and tired,
> And vigorous young men stumble badly,
> Yet those who wait for the Lord
> Will gain new strength;
> They will mount up with wings like eagles,
> They will run and not get tired,
> They will walk and not become weary. *(vv. 28-31)*

This is the God who has made a love-commitment to you. This is the God who has accepted you as His child; who has called Himself your Father.

Our Response

Seeing God as He presents Himself calls out a unique response from us. It invites us to a totally new approach to life—an approach that seems to be one of utter foolishness to those who see life with God left out. Matthew 6:25-34 describes this lifestyle; one marked by total dependence.

Matthew 6:25. Jesus begins by presenting a deed to freedom. "Do not be anxious for your life, as to what you shall eat, or what you shall drink; nor for your body, as to what you shall put on." This isn't saying that these physical needs are *unimportant*. It is saying that we are no longer to be anxious about them.

Matthew 6:26. How are we freed from such anxious feelings? Christ points to the birds. God has so designed the world that their needs are met, even though they are unable to plan ahead and care for themselves. And, He adds, "Your heavenly Father feeds them." Even though the birds aren't His children, His care extends to them. You *are* children to Him. "Are you not worth much more than they?"

This is critical in helping us learn to depend on God. Let's realize that our Father will care for us all the days of our lives.

Matthew 6:31-32. Jesus again proclaims our freedom. "Do not be anxious then." Others who do not know God will worry about *things,* hoping to find in them the security and peace for which they yearn. But for you and me, knowing God as Father, there is another source of security entirely. "Your heavenly

Father knows that you need all these things."

And *you* know your heavenly Father!

Dependence

Coming to view God as completely trustworthy and learning to depend on Him does bring us an amazing sense of security. With our anxiety relieved, we're free to concentrate on the real meaning of life for us. With dependence comes a new direction for life, and a promise.

The direction? "Seek first His kingdom" (Matt. 6:33). Seek first of all for His will to be all that matters to you.

The promise? "And all these things shall be added to you." God your Father will not fail you. He does love you, and He does have all power.

GOING DEEPER

1. What was your father like? In what ways do you feel he was like God the Father? In what ways was he unlike Him? Share with your friend(s).
2. Which factor seems most significant to you in helping you see God as truly trustworthy?
    - understanding dependence
    - assurance of God's love
    - assurance of God's power

   Discuss why you selected this factor.
3. Look over the Isaiah passage, thought by thought. What image of God does it project? What is the impact on you?
4. For memorization: Matthew 6:25-31.
5. Bible study: Psalm 103; Luke 15:11-32.

11 Jesus, Our Saviour

He was a very troubled man, this Joseph. He wanted to do the right thing. He had a warm and true affection for the Jewish teen-ager he was to marry. Yet, she'd been found pregnant. He knew he ought to denounce her. But it was so out of character for her; so far from all he knew about her.

As Joseph struggled with his dilemma, God resolved it. An angel appeared to Joseph in a dream, encouraging him to accept Mary as his wife and explaining that hers was a supernatural conception, "for that which is conceived in her is of the Holy Ghost" (Matt. 1:20). To this young virgin, a Son would be born. He would be named Jesus, "for it is He who will save His people from their sins" (Matt. 1:21).

This announcement freed Joseph from his dilemma. Even before His birth, Jesus had begun a ministry of deliverance!

Today too this announcement is the charter of your freedom and of mine. Name Him Jesus. It is He who will save His people from their sins.

The Meaning of His Name

The name "Jesus" was not uncommon in Israel. In Hebrew the name is "Joshua," and means "deliverer." Like the Old Testament Joshua, who led the people of Israel into the Promised Land and delivered them from the years of wilderness wandering, this newborn infant was to have a ministry defined by His name.

He was to be a deliverer.

He was to deliver His people—from their sins.

Earlier, when we looked at guilt and forgiveness, we received some insight into why you and I need deliverance. *Sin,* we saw, refers to acts that flow both from our imperfection and from our willful choice of evil. Yet sin is more than acts. Sin is the warping of our personality that makes us incomplete, and that makes us desire evil. Salvation, or deliverance, from sin involves more than "making up" for past faults. It must also involve the cleansing and reshaping of our personality. Salvation has to deal with guilt, yes—but it also has to deal with that trait in us that disposes us toward sinful acts.

When the angel announced, "His name is Deliverer," and went on to explain, "He will save His people from their sins," the angel was conveying God's announcement of a truly massive intervention into human experience. Jesus does more than send away guilt. He deals with our sin!

When we understand how He deals with sin, we'll know more of what it means for us to have Him as Saviour, and more of what it means to be a Christian. We'll see, too, why Jesus *has to be* God. Only God can possibly be powerful enough not only to forgive, but to break sin's power within us, and ultimately to free us from its very presence.

Sins Past

There's nothing we can do about past sins. We have a saying we use to help us shrug off the past: "No use crying over spilt milk." Yet, sin in our past isn't so easily dismissed. Not only does it make us feel guilty and ashamed, but also our sinful choices have changed the direction of our lives. One can't say to an alcoholic dying of liver disease, "No use crying over spilt milk!" One can't say to a man on the edge of divorce, "No use crying over spilt milk."

I met Verl when I was employed at a mental hospital in Michigan, working my way through the university. He had been sent to the hospital from jail, where he had tried to commit suicide by cutting his wrists. I held a Bible class in our ward each evening, and one night after class Verl asked to talk with me in private. There I learned his story.

He'd had his own business, been a member of his local church and even Sunday School superintendent. When the war came, he'd begun to work at the aircraft plant at Willow Run. One day he had gone to a young woman's home to sell a ring, and from then on his life had drastically changed. Verl made a choice there, a willful choice of what he knew was wrong.

Everything changed then. Verl took up drinking, and, being a very handsome man, soon found other women. With the war over, he went back to his small business. There he systematically cheated his customers and lied on his tax returns. His wife and his teen-age children became strangers to him—just people he lived with but cared nothing for compared to his pleasures.

Then one day his neighbor had come home early, and found Verl in bed with his wife. The neighbor turned around, went to the corner bar, and began to tell everyone what he'd found.

Suddenly, inexplicably, Verl couldn't face himself any more. This was the last straw for his wife too. She determined to leave him. The teens, ashamed and angry, urged her on. Verl took all the money from their joint account and headed west. Then he began to work his way back toward home, drinking in town after town. Finally, months later, he was picked up and jailed as a drunk in his home city, and in ultimate despair made the suicide attempt.

Sin in Verl's past had given his life its tragic and heartbreaking direction. Who could say to Verl, "No use crying over spilt milk"? It was his *life* that had been spilled! His life, and the countless tears of his family and friends.

That afternoon Verl told me his story—and something more. He'd been coming to the Bible class regularly for two weeks. Now he said, "Larry, I believe God let me get to the very bottom because I wouldn't listen to Him. But now I've come back to the Lord—really come back—and I know I'm forgiven."

The guilt of the sins that were past had been sent away by Jesus' forgiveness.

But what about the pain? Later, Verl asked me to write to his wife and tell her what God had done for him. His wife, who had remained faithful to the Lord through all the pain-wracked years, couldn't believe that God had finally reached her husband. So I wrote, and shared my conviction that Verl truly was a renewed man. How hard it was for her. Finally she replied. He could come home, but she couldn't bear the thought of living with him as his wife. He could come home; the children could use a father. But that was all.

I shook hands with Verl when he left and wished him well. About 8 weeks later, I received a brief letter—a letter I carried with me for years until it wore away. Verl told me that he'd gone back to his business. He'd gone back to his church. He'd gone back to his family and to his neighborhood. It was hard, he wrote, but he was living now just to show everyone what a change God can make in a man's life. Already some (including his wife) were beginning to see how real Jesus is.

The guilt of sins past had been forgiven. Now a life that had been spoiled and wasted was being rebuilt, and the pain was being healed by the touch of Jesus' transforming love.

Jesus is the Saviour we need for our past sins. We need forgiveness to wash out our sense of guilt and the guilt itself. And we need His power, to rebuild a life that has been twisted and deformed. And how we need grace, to reach out and touch again with love the people that our sin has hurt and bruised! With Jesus as Saviour, our past can be changed in ways that we might have believed impossible.

How joyously we can say with David the psalmist, "Blessed are those whose lawless deeds have been forgiven, and whose sins have been covered. Blessed is the man whose sin the Lord will not take into account" (Rom. 4:7-8; see Ps. 32:1-2). How blessed *we* are. In Jesus we have a Saviour who deals with sins past.

Present Sin

Recently my boys and I went up to the Colorado River near Bullhead City to fish for striped bass. We got our small, 12-foot boat in the water and sped downstream as evening fell, finding the river fishing very different than we expected. Finally, I turned the bow of the boat upstream to return to our car —and was jolted to find that we weren't moving! I had our 7½ horsepower motor wide open, but the current was so swift that we could barely hold our own.

How much like the sin within us! Like an awesome current, sin pounds into us, constantly tugging and pulling, clawing at us until it threatens to sweep us along by its power. Too often we are unable to resist its swift downstream flow. All the power within our personalities seems at best able only to hold us briefly against it. And, oh, how easy to slip, and find ourselves carried along and away.

Yet, in presenting Jesus as Saviour, the Bible promises you and me the power to move *upstream*. The current will always be there during our earthly life. The tug will always be present within us. But Jesus will be with us too—freeing us from the kind of dilemma my boys and I faced. With Jesus present, the current need not sweep us away, or even hold us back!

Romans 6 explores what Jesus as Saviour means in your present struggle with sin. Let's look.

Romans 6:1-2. Some have reacted to the message of God's unconditional forgiveness by suggesting that, if salvation is so "easy," what's to keep us from sinning? In fact, why not sin *more,* to give God more to forgive thus showing how great His grace is? Paul rejects this thought with horror, pointing out that in Jesus we have "died to sin," and are not to live in it any longer.

This idea of "dead to sin" is a key to understanding what Jesus means to you as daily Saviour.

Romans 6:3. Paul begins to explore this concept

by pointing out that all who have been "baptized into Christ" have been "baptized into His death." This baptism is not water baptism, but the reality that water baptism symbolizes. The root idea of "baptize" is to "be identified with." Thus the Bible says that when you and I became Christians through faith in Christ, the Holy Spirit united us with Him in a real union (1 Cor. 12:13). We became part of His body, and were thus joined to Him who is the Head. *We are identified with Jesus because we are united to Him.*

And, Paul says, we were united with Him "in His death."

Romans 6:4-5. This point is now developed. Jesus died, was buried, and then "raised from the dead through the glory of the Father." *And we have been united to Jesus in all this.* The result? We too may walk in newness of life. Our "old self," that part of our personality that is in sin's swift current and so easily swept along, was crucified with Him, in order that it might be rendered inoperative in our daily life.

Think of a powerful motor in a car. You turn on the ignition, and the engine growls with life. When you shift to *Drive,* that motor will hurtle your car along the highway. But when you're in *Neutral,* no matter how the engine may roar, its power is not transmitted to the wheels.

This passage is not saying that, as Christians, sin's engine will be removed from our lives. It's saying that through Jesus' death (and your death with Him), sin's engine has been thrown into *Neutral!* It can growl and roar all it will, even shaking the car. But unless you choose to shift into sin's gear, the power of sin will no longer hurtle you through life! Sin has been done away with as the controlling aspect of our bodily lives "that we should no longer be slaves to sin."

Romans 6:11-13. How do we experience this freedom? By counting on the Saviour, *now*.

The passage goes on to teach that you and I really are "dead to sin" in that its pull need not carry us along any more. We'll feel the pull, but let's not get frightened by it. We are free to "not let sin rule" in us. We need to make God a present of all we are now, and let Him use us as instruments of His righteousness

Because Jesus is Saviour from sin *present* as well as sin *past,* you need not choose to sin. You don't need to live on the level of your imperfection. You can live a new life, in which God takes all you are and infuses you with His life and with His righteousness.

It was this kind of deliverance that Verl was thinking of when he wrote me that letter from his home. It was hard. But living in the very currents that had torn him away from God and swept him toward death, Verl was demonstrating the power of God to change human experience.

That power to change is yours and mine today. However difficult it is for us, whatever the pressure, Jesus is Saviour for you, right now.

Sin Future

Sin's impact has been felt by all of creation. Pollution, corruption, and deterioration have marked the physical universe as well as our moral experience. The world God created and pronounced "good" is a far different world than the one we know now (see Gen. 3:17-18). And we are different too. We've known hurt and pain, alienation and guilt, shame and bitterness, prejudice and injury, war and poverty. Sin has warped not only the individual but all of society.

Does Jesus as Saviour, as the One who "will save His people from their sins," speak to this too?

The Bible is clear that Jesus does speak to all of creation and to society. In Romans, Paul envisions the creation itself set free from its slavery to corruption, breaking into the "freedom of the glory of the children of God" (Rom. 8:21). In providing salvation to us, God through Jesus touches *everything* with healing grace.

We don't know a lot about that future. We do know there will be a new heaven and earth, "wherein dwelleth righteousness." We see dim sketches of a whole and healthy society (Isa. 65). And, beyond time, we see eternity stretching out in endless and purified existence (Rev. 21). We see ourselves, freed not only from the power but even the presence of sin. "We shall be like Him," the Bible promises, "for we shall see Him just as He is." How good to know that while it does not yet appear what we shall be," we'll be like Jesus! (1 John 3:2-3) The end toward which our life is moving, Christlikeness, will be fully realized.

This too is what Jesus, Saviour, means for us. We know that the day is coming when we will be forever and totally free.

Someday Verl will stand with Jesus, and then it will all be past. There will be no remembered guilt for him. There will be no struggle to disregard the sin that surges within. There will be only harmony, and peace and the dynamic freedom to experience all that we yearn to be. With all past, we'll look at Jesus, and with awe and full understanding, realize what it means for Him to be our Saviour.

GOING DEEPER

1. What difference has knowing Jesus as Saviour made in your past and present? Share any specifics you feel free to with your friend(s).
2. Read Romans 6:1-14, using several modern translations and paraphrases. If you want to explore it further, use a good commentary, such as James M. Stifler's one-volume *Epistle to the Romans* (Moody Press), or Donald Grey Barnhouse's several-volume study. It is really important to grasp what Jesus, as Saviour now, means to you.
3. For a memory challenge this week, why not take on the whole Romans 6:1-14 passage? There's truth here you'll really want to know and take to heart.
4. Bible study: Isaiah 65; Revelation 20—21.

12 | The Holy Spirit, Our Companion

Last night was Tuesday, so 23 of us gathered to study and share We studied Philippians 2, the chapter that tells about Jesus' example of humility and total submission to God's will. And we concentrated on verses 12 and 13; I paraphrased them this way:

> Attack your difficulties with confidence and a due sense of responsibility, for God is at work in you, expressing His will in every situation as you keep your life in focus through obedience (something you excelled in while I was there, and need to concentrate on even more now that I am gone).

We had an exciting time of sharing. Several had been blessed to realize that the phrase in the regular translation, "to will and to do His good purpose," promises that God will even shape our desires. He'll help us *want to* do what we feel we ought to do! John, the new Christian I mentioned in chapter 3, was a real blessing again. He told how he had been learning to look at his difficulties with the confidence that, if God does not work things out the way he wants, then God must be doing something better.

John is really coming to believe that God is expressing His will in every situation.

At the end of our time together, we began to share the most important thing each of us had learned from God through this passage.

Then it happened. A visitor to our group, who had been quiet all evening, began to talk. "Something I haven't heard all evening, but a line of teaching expressed throughout the whole Bible, concerns the Holy Spirit. It isn't mentioned here, but. . . ." He went on to talk for several minutes in generalities about the Holy Spirit, making no attempt to relate Him to the text or to our earlier sharing. I have to confess I was disturbed. We had been sharing what God taught us in a passage that directs our attention to Jesus Christ. God's Word hadn't introduced the Spirit. Why, when we were talking about Jesus, should attention be drawn to the Spirit?

I share this because, as we begin to deal with this Person of the Trinity, the Holy Spirit, who is our constant Companion, we need to understand something about Him that may seem strange. It's something Jesus said to His disciples. "When He, the Spirit of truth, comes, He will guide you into all the truth; for He will not speak on His own initiative, but whatever He hears, He will speak; and He will disclose to you what is to come. *He shall glorify Me,* for He shall take of Mine, and shall disclose it unto you" (John 16:13-14). The Holy Spirit has come to be with us and guide us—and what he communicates will be Jesus' personal message. His whole ministry will concentrate on glorifying Jesus, and making Him the center of our attention and our praise.

Recently I met a husband-wife team. She sings, ne works the music tapes and cares for the details of their appearances. When you talk with him, he's very quick to take attention off his part of their shared ministry and bring it back to her. Everything he does in the ministry they share is designed to help *her* communicate. When she sings, he's in the background, unseen but essential.

The relationship between Jesus and the Spirit is similar. The Spirit's part of the Godhead's shared ministry is vital. But it is designed to help Jesus communicate. He "takes of Mine," Jesus said, "and shall disclose it unto you." When God the Holy Spirit ministers in us, He always keeps our eyes focused on Jesus.

That's why I was disturbed last night with our visitor's approach. He was trying to take our attention *off* Jesus, where the Holy Spirit wants it, and put it on the Spirit. That is *not* God's intention. And it's not healthy for us!

In Balance

Somehow we need to keep in balance our thinking about the Holy Spirit. On the one hand, we want to be aware of His presence and His gifts to us. And we want to give Him praise as God. On the other hand, we don't want to make the Holy Spirit the focus of our faith, or to so emphasize His gifts that we begin to feel that He, rather than Jesus, sets us apart and makes us brothers and sisters. Jesus is the center of our lives. He is the source of our unity. When we shift that center to the Spirit, or make His gifts a core for unity, we have definitely drifted away from God's intention. And there is no doubt that we have made the Spirit uncomfortable as well. He wants our attention on Jesus, not on Him.

Balance, then, is important. With it, we also need

a clear understanding of just how great a gift the Holy Spirit's presence is. So, let's survey a few passages that tell us about our great Companion.

God's gift. This is the first, exciting thing about the Holy Spirit. He is the Father's gift to us. Jesus told His disciples on the crucifixion eve, "I tell you the truth, it is to your advantage that I go away; for if I do not go away, the Helper shall not come to you; but if I go, I will send Him to you" (John 16:7). It was better for them (and for us) that God the Holy Spirit come than that the Son stay!

The Spirit's name here is important: *Helper.* Sometimes translated *Comforter,* the term means in the original to *stand alongside.* Jesus' leaving didn't mean that His followers were to be deserted. Far from it. After Jesus' resurrection and ascension, God the Holy Spirit was sent as our permanent Companion. In the Person of the Holy Spirit, God takes His stand with us. He is *here.* In every situation, the Helper we need to give us strength and wisdom is with us!

This is the first thing to know. God the Holy Spirit is your constant Companion, standing with you, eager to provide the help you need.

Yours, now. Sometimes we find it hard to grasp. God has given Himself to us. Doubting, we revert to our old ways and attitudes, and begin to feel that we have to do something to merit such a gift. Certainly we ought at least to *tarry*—to beg God for the gift, and wait steadfastly for it. At least, this is what some feel

But remember our earlier chapters? Remember that God says, "How shall He not freely with Him [Jesus], give us all things?" God's way of relating to us is in grace. God intends to give freely. This is just what He has done in giving us the Spirit!

Romans 8:9 puts it clearly. "If anyone does not have the Spirit of Christ, he does not belong to Him." And, yet more positively, 1 Corinthians 12 shows that each believer not only has the Holy Spirit with Him, he also has a Spirit-given gift! Upon our conversion, the Holy Spirit came to us, and He Himself became the link that joins us to Jesus and each other (1 Cor. 12:13). You don't have to *ask* for the Spirit, or beg. The Holy Spirit is with you now, and He'll stay with you as a divine pledge that you will always be God's child: a divine Presence to let you know that you are a most precious possession of your heavenly Father (Eph. 1:13-14).

And to be your Helper.

His concerns. Why has the Spirit come to be your Companion? What does He intend to do in you? Scripture speaks revealingly.

(1) *Of fruit.* Galatians speaks of the fruit that the Holy Spirit produces in our lives. On the list are "love, joy, peace, patience, kindness, goodness, faithfulness, gentleness, self-control" (Gal. 5:22-23). God has always been concerned more with who we are than with what we do. He has announced His intention to reshape us until we are like Jesus in character and love. Isn't it striking that Jesus told His disciples, "love each other,"—and then spoke of His love as the model? The love the Spirit produces in us *is* Jesus' love. So too Jesus said we would know *His* joy (John 17:13) and *His* peace (John 14:27).

Do you wonder if the Spirit is in your life? Quiet the doubts, first by confidence that what God promises must be true. And then by seeing in your growing love and joy and peace sure evidence of His working in your inner life.

(2) *Of guidance.* The Holy Spirit also teaches us opening our minds to the Word and bringing to mind

truths we need to apply as we live (John 14:26). In this ministry, He is called our Counselor.

Glenna was excited last night because during the week she had seen in Philippians 2:13 the promise that God would give her a desire to do what she felt she should do. God was at work to "will" in her as well as to "do" His good purposes. All during the week she kept remembering. Remembering, and praying, and experiencing that truth.

Who brought her that insight? Who reminded her to apply the truth she'd seen? It was her constant Companion, the Holy Spirit, quietly counseling and guiding her through the days of her life.

He didn't focus her attention on Himself. Not at all. He focused her attention on Jesus. Yet because of the Spirit's ministry, Glenna knew a week marked by Jesus' joy.

(3) *Of ministry.* Another unique work of the Holy Spirit is to *minister through us.* This ministry is both to non-Christians with whom we share the Gospel (John 16:8-11), and to believers, as we share through the spiritual gifts He has given (1 Cor. 12; Romans 12). This is a very liberating thing to realize. The response of a person to what we share doesn't depend on us. It's not how well we speak, or how convincingly we argue. God's work is done only as the Holy Spirit takes our words and uses them in the hearts and minds of others. God the Holy Spirit can take even our poor efforts (or even our best!) and work His own miracles in people's lives.

It's just the same with the edifying gifts—the special abilities that God gives each of us to use to build up other believers. The Holy Spirit is the One who takes what we say and do and makes it effective. So we're free to share. We don't need to draw back, afraid that we're not skilled enough, or that we will cloud the issue. When we're prompted by His voice to speak, counting on Him as our constant Companion, we can speak—and can leave the results to Him.

(4) *Of enablement.* The Bible often speaks of God as enabling us and providing strength. It was the Spirit who applied the benefits of Jesus' death to us to give us new life; now He stays with us to strengthen us and energize us (Rom. 8:11). There is so much we simply can't do. If we're honest with ourselves, we know our limitations. How good then to face a challenge with confidence, to *know* that God is at work in us to will and do His good purpose! We can count on the Holy Spirit. He is with us. He will enable us—providing the wisdom and strength we need to do His will.

These, then, are things that the Bible tells us God cares about in our lives. And these are the things that the Holy Spirit concentrates on. His ministry is focused on our transformation. On guiding us, ministering through us, and giving us the strength to do His will. In all of these ministries, He directs our attention to Jesus. In each of them He glorifies Jesus. It is Jesus' joy and peace and goodness that He produces in us, and it is Jesus that others begin to see in us.

This Holy Spirit is with you always.

This Holy Spirit is at work in you now, and you can count on His presence and companionship.

Yet the Holy Spirit remains "off stage." The spotlight is always on Jesus, and our eyes are to be on Jesus too.

Tongues?

This is an issue I'd like to skip. For one thing, entire

books have been given to exploring it. Little new can be said here. Besides, fixing attention on this miraculous gift of the Spirit or others like it really does not help us in our daily growth or our experience of God's best.

Still, there is a great emphasis on the Holy Spirit and tongues in some circles today ("tongues" being the speaking in a tongue unknown to speaker and listener). According to some, such supernatural manifestations had a specific function in the Early Church before the Bible was completed. And they terminated at that point. Others insist that supernatural gifts are in fact *the* mark of the Spirit's presence, and that those who have not "spoken in tongues" don't have Him, and are at best second-class Christians.

There's room for debate over whether such gifts as tongues ceased with the close of Apostolic times. Yet it should be clear that God is free to give such gifts again if He so chooses. I think all of us should hesitate to label the experience of a brother or sister who knows and loves Jesus as "demonic" or "a delusion."

But at the same time, we can say with assurance that such manifestations are *not* "the" mark of the Spirit's presence. Nor are they necessary for full experience of all God has for us in Christ. The Bible makes clear that the Spirit's ministries focus on Jesus. The Bible also makes clear that the Holy Spirit is God's gift to each believer: He *is* your constant Companion.

Any persons or movements that seek to make the Holy Spirit the focus of attention, or insist that some supposed manifestation of His presence provides a basis for fellowship, are clearly out of harmony with what God says of the Spirit and His work. The

Spirit's major concern is with our transformation, with His ministry in our personality and through us to others. This emphasis is clear in 1 Corinthians 14, as summarized in verse 12: "Since you are so anxious to have special gifts from the Holy Spirit, ask Him for the very best, for those that will be of real help to the whole church" (LB). If you really want to see Him work in your life, concentrate, with Him, on helping others grow in Christ.

In a way, whether there are valid "tongues" today isn't all that important. God gives the various manifestations of the Spirit to believers as He chooses—giving some one, others another of His gifts (1 Cor. 12:4-17). Rather than being upset about something we're supposedly missing, let's concentrate on what God *has* given us, and realize that this is His great blessing for us. Let's count on what God says we have been given in the Person of the Holy Spirit: God Himself, come to take His stand with us as our Companion.

This, I think, is what most disturbs me about the emphasis some lay on the Spirit. In urging others to "get" the Spirit (and prove it by speaking in tongues), they deny His presence in the believer. And it's so important to know we have the Spirit to count on.

It's important to know you're not alone.

It's important to know that you're not a second-class Christian—that God has, in Jesus, given you His very best.

It's important to know the Holy Spirit is with you now, that He is someone constantly but unobtrusively at work in your life, keeping your attention on Jesus, helping you trust and obey.

It's important to know that you can step out in confidence to meet life daily, sure that your constant

Companion is there, providing guidance, inner peace, power for ministry, strength to meet every need.

This is just what God wants you to count on.

>   His presence with you.
>   His love for you.
>   His power in you.

How good to know that, with God as your Father, with Jesus as your Saviour, with the Spirit as your Companion, your life from now on *will be new*.

GOING DEEPER

1. Have you ever felt abandoned as a Christian? Share that experience with your friend(s).
2. Think about that experience again, and this time apply what we've been saying. What difference would it have made if you had been fully convinced in that situation that the Holy Spirit was with you? What would have changed? What would not have changed?
3. Review the several ministries of the Spirit that this chapter suggests. Which of these would you have needed most in the situation above?
4. Using a concordance, look up New Testament references to the Holy Spirit. Select two to memorize which you find particularly meaningful.
5. Bible study: 1 Corinthians 12—14.